Toward a New Earth:
Apocalypse in the American Novel

Toward a New Earth:
Apocalypse in
the American Novel

JOHN R. MAY

UNIVERSITY OF NOTRE DAME PRESS
Notre Dame   London

Grateful acknowledgment is made to the editors of *Studies in Short Fiction, Renascence*, and *Twentieth Century Literature* for permission to reprint material that appeared in those journals in slightly different form. Section 3 of chapter 2 appeared in *Studies in Short Fiction* 8, no. 3 (Summer 1971), pp. 411–22, as "The Gospel According to Philip Traum: Structural Unity in 'The Mysterious Stranger.'" Chapter 4 appeared in *Renascence* 23, no. 1 (Autumn 1970), pp. 31–45, as "Images of Apocalypse in the Black Novel." The portion of chapter 5 dealing with *Cat's Cradle* appeared in *Twentieth Century Literature* 18, no. 1 (January 1972), pp. 25–36, as part of an article entitled "Vonnegut's Humor and the Limits of Hope."

Library of Congress Catalog Card Number: 72-3510
Manufactured in the United States of America

ACKNOWLEDGMENTS

Who can decide where indebtedness begins when influence upon a book is in question, especially if the work reflects a theological vision and a love of literature that have merged with personal growth over the years? I recall with gratitude not only my family and friends who shared with me the vision of faith and the pleasure of literature but also my many teachers and mentors who provided a critical basis for the acceptance of faith and the appreciation of literature.

I am deeply grateful to the faculty of the Institute of Liberal Arts at Emory University, who offered an atmosphere of continuing encouragement and challenge throughout the work on this book; particularly, to David H. Hesla, for his invaluable direction of the whole project and his reassuring sense of interdisciplinary method; to William B. Dillingham, for his wise insistence upon a close reading of the literary text and for enthusiastically imparting an awareness of its value; to William A. Beardslee, for his gracious help in sharpening the historical treatment of apocalypse and for his contagious sensitivity to our Puritan heritage; to Robert

Detweiler, for his critical reading of the manuscript and his probing bibliographical questions.

Finally, I wish to thank Ann Rice for her editorial assistance and Servando Mendez, S.J., the closest of friends, for sharing with me so often the distress and the humor of proofreading as well as of life.

CONTENTS

Then he who sat on the throne said, 'Behold! I am making all things new!' (And he said to me, 'Write this down; for these words are trustworthy and true.')

Rev. 21:5

CHAPTER ONE

Apocalypse and
the American Tradition

The Christian imagination is essentially an imagination of promise, an openness to the present because of the possibilities that it unfolds, a refusal to seek escape from the ravages of time through any subterfuge—either through nostalgia for the past or by flight into the timeless world of aesthetic or "religious" experience. The Christian imagination is grounded in history, aware of the irreversibility of time, anxious for the fulfillment of its dreams.

Yet to speak of hope and promise as the core of the Christian message is to use a language of eschatology that is peculiar to our age. Only within the past few decades has Christian man, through his consciousness of space-time in an evolving universe, expressed his eschatological self-awareness in terms of the hope of history and the promise of the world. In the words of Jürgen Moltmann, this is an age of "'creative expectation,' [of] hope which sets about criticizing and transforming the present because it is open towards the universal future of the kingdom."[1] Only within this period has Christian man understood the promise of grace as making him more human. For whether one speaks in terms of the call to authentic existence (Bultmann) or of hominization and personalization (Teilhard de Chardin), one is using an eschatological language peculiar to the contemporary world.

The theological literary critic, insisting upon the autonomy of literature yet sensitive to its possible religious dimensions, is faced with a complex task of historical evaluation. To search for the literary analogue of the present Christian understanding of the world in the literature of an earlier period is to confess a basic misunderstanding of the historical conditioning of language: The theologian critic simply cannot use contemporary language for interpreting the eschatological literature of former periods. On the other hand, language traditions have a way of surviving their period of currency, so it should be clear from the outset that earlier eschatological language may endure into the present.

The purpose of this work, therefore, will be to derive from literary and theological sources a typology representing the various eschatological language traditions in their successive historical phases. Since apocalypse is the most poetic and imaginative form of eschatological writing, it will serve as the theological basis for the typology. And because I hope primarily to contribute to an interpretation of the acknowledged strand of American literary apocalypse, chapters 2 through 5 represent an empirical approach to the analysis of the variations and innovations in apocalyptic form in American literature. The theological criticism of literature, always extrinsic to the literary evaluation of the work, depends in the final analysis, though, on such an attempt as this to construct a typology based on historical language traditions, however modest the heuristic role one may attribute to the results.[2]

Myths of the end of the world are apparently as old as man's active religious imagination, yet it was only a quarter of a century ago that the description of apocalypse became historical, as Perry Miller has so wryly pointed out. Quoting from the official *United States Bombing Survey* the factual description of the effects of the atomic blast at Hiroshima, he observes:

> The authors . . . are not, I am persuaded, theologians or poets, and they probably did not know that they were falling into the pattern of a literary form more ancient, and more rigid, than the sonnet. Yet a hundred artists of the apocalyptic vision would envy them the stark simplicity, as well as the perfect tense, of their summation: "The atomic bomb shattered the normal fabric of community life and disrupted the organizations for handling the disaster."[3]

Miller speaks of artistic envy of the "perfect tense" because he seems to feel that a desire to end it all is innate to man, as if overwhelmed by the ravages of time man projects onto the macrocosm his own desire for personal surcease. How seriously we are to take his estimate is one thing; whether it is supported by the history of religions is another altogether. There would seem to be no other sure way, though, of coming to a deeper understanding of the historical traditions of apocalypse

than by taking the long and arduous path that begins
with primitive man and winds its way through the
modifications of the Judaeo-Christian experience before
reaching the often purely secular motif of American
apocalypse.

My purpose here also is to discern what elements of
these language traditions have been and still are so universally true of the apocalyptic form that they can be
said to be essential to its purpose and meaning and thus
serve as a canon for describing contemporary American variations. Some of the questions that will have to
be answered are the following: How and why did primitive man imagine cosmic catastrophe (insofar as this
can be discerned from extant myth and ritual)? How
does Judaeo-Christian apocalyptic literature compare
with the more general myths of man? What factors in
the American experience have contributed to the strong
tradition for apocalypse in its literature? Why does
modern man's anxiety about the end often seem so thoroughly pessimistic? It is not hard to understand how a
world that has survived two catastrophic global wars
and that lives daily with the imminent possibility of
nuclear cataclysm could have produced the literature
of anxiety that we accept as ours. And even though the
imagination of cosmic catastrophe is nothing new to
man, it is true that the dawning of the thermonuclear
age, when man has developed the literal capacity to
destroy the world himself, has added something of a
cutting edge to the anxiety spawned by the literary,
artistic, and even religious imagination of contemporary
man. Although our investigation conforms to a histor-

ical pattern, the nature of the material is such that the historical references to religious belief will frequently best be clarified by contrast with the modern temper.

I

In *Myth and Reality*, Mircea Eliade notes the widespread incidence of myths of cosmic cataclysm among primitive peoples, especially where the cataclysm is accepted as having occurred sometime in the past of the race.[4] The instrument of destruction—whether it is fire, flood, or earthquake—represents a return to chaos followed by a new creation. The cataclysm is usually attributed either to the sins of mankind or to the decrepitude of the world. These myths of past catastrophe are taken by Eliade to be projections onto a macrocosmic scale of the "return to origins" of the primitive New Year festival, where—as in the Babylonian *akitu* ritual—the celebration of the end of the world is an annual affair. Eliade explains:

> The extinction of fires, the return of the souls of the dead, social confusion of the type exemplified by the Saturnalia, erotic license, orgies, and so on, symbolized the retrogression of the cosmos into chaos. On the last day of the year the universe was dissolved in the primordial waters. The marine monster Tiamat—symbol of darkness, of the formless, the non-manifested—revived and once again threatened. The world that had existed for the whole year *really* disappeared. Since Tiamat was again present, the cosmos was annulled; and Marduk was obliged to create it once again, after having once again conquered Tiamat.[5]

Aside from the fact that this ritual progression from chaos to cosmogony is a religious celebration and is considered by primitives to represent contact with reality itself—an important consideration that we will have to return to shortly—it should be clear that these myths of past cataclysm are basically optimistic in nature. There is no chaos without a new creation.

Myths of future cataclysm are apparently scarce among primitive peoples (Eliade admits that our lack of information in this area is attributable possibly to ethnologists' failure to ask this question), and those that omit the possibility of re-creation are practically nonexistent. American Indians possessed myths built upon a cyclic pattern of destruction and re-creation, or expected a new creation that would come about even without cataclysm. According to the Indian understanding of the ages of the world, the cyclic pattern of creation, deterioration, destruction, and re-creation is basically hopeful in structure at least in that it knows re-creation and reincarnation, even though the Indian desires to escape from the terrors of the cosmic cycle through mystical experience. There is a millennialism that has been developing among contemporary primitives that is built upon cataclysm and the expectation of a new age; and all of these myths are understandably antiwhite and antichristian, representing a revolt against the failure of missionaries to live their religion.

The meanings assigned to these myths are interesting and highly instructive to our basic investigation. First of all—and this is obviously Mircea Eliade's overworked but nonetheless perceptive thesis—primitive man sought to protect himself from the ravages of profane time by periodic reenactment of the cosmogony which itself constituted contact with sacred time, the time of the gods and of man's origin. But, as Eliade has pointed out, this mythical ritual was not primitive man's way of burying his head in the sand, of saying No to reality. Because of his vision of the way things are, the repetition of the chaos-to-cosmogony ritual was his way of affirming what he considered to be reality itself: "The desire felt by the man of traditional societies to refuse history, and to confine himself to an indefinite repetition of archetypes, testifies to his thirst for the real and his terror of 'losing' himself by letting himself be overwhelmed by the meaninglessness of profane existence. . . . This behavior corresponds to a desperate effort not to lose contact with *being*."[6]

In addition to representing contact with being itself, the repetition of the mythic ritual of re-creation had the purifying effect of abolishing the past and its sins and of beginning life afresh. The implications here for the Judaeo-Christian experience seem quite obvious. The call of the prophets, most especially of Jesus, is to a change of heart that necessitates rejection of the past and its failures before a new life can be embraced.

Thus there is implied in the archaic ritual not only a denial of the past and its failures but also an affirmation of man's creative capacity to start anew, in the pattern of the divine exemplar. Eliade universalizes this relationship between chaos and creativity: "Creativity is always found in relation to some 'madness' or 'orgy' involved with the symbolism of death and darkness."[7] In speaking

of the symbolic entrance into the belly of the monster
as a ritual of initiation, Eliade insists that it is "equivalent to a regression into the primal indistinctness, into
the cosmic Night—and to come out of the monster is
equivalent to a cosmogony: it is to pass from Chaos to
Creation. . . . Every initiatory adventure of this type
ends in the *creation* of something, in the founding of a
new world or a new mode of being."[8] Again, while discussing the assumed madness of the future shaman, he
insists that *"the symbolic return to chaos is indispensable
to any new creation; . . . it is a sign that the profane man
is on the way to dissolution, and that a new personality
is about to be born."*[9] Thus the achievement of wisdom
and for that matter of any sacred or creative knowledge
is always seen as the fruit of such a process of initiation.
Finally, there is more than a suggestion that the ritual
participation in chaos was also a way of gaining power
over the frightening reality of death, of putting it in its
perspective, so that it "ceased to present itself as a *cessa-
tion* and became a *rite of passage*."[10]

Insofar as primitive man seeks to contact reality and
participate in the sacred by imitating the divine models,
there is implicit in the repetition of the cyclic pattern
an acknowledgment of man's failure to live according
to the prescribed pattern. What makes the mythic ritual
so eminently worth repeating is the fact that it embodies
the perfect mode of conduct. In Eliade's now classic
definition, myth is the sacred history of what transpired
in the beginning, "in a primordial and non-temporal
instant, a moment of *sacred time*."[11] And because it is
sacred, it is also absolutely true and real (the only valid

revelation of reality), and thus also the exemplary pattern for human behavior. By imitating the exemplary acts of the gods or of the mythic hero, man transcends profane time and enters into sacred time itself.[12]

The abolition of the past which we discussed above as a motive for the ritual repetition of the primordial chaos must be seen, therefore, in relationship to these patterns for human activity provided by the divine exemplars. The judgment implicit in the repetition of the ritual is expiated only by the initiatory passage through death to new life, through chaos to new creation.

Eliade's understanding of the function of myth in human existence is clearly germane to our investigation of the historical variations of the symbolism of catastrophe and renewal. Some attempt must be made, though, to explicate the cluster of terms related to his explanation of the significance of myth since Eliade himself avoids outright definition. A myth for Eliade is composed of interrelated symbols or images which themselves represent autonomous modes of human cognition and as such are "consubstantial with human existence."[13] For example, the myth of the end of the world, or among primitive peoples of the periodic repetition of the cosmogony, is made up of related symbols of chaos and creation, the particular symbol varying with the culture that has created the myth. Darkness, the extinction of fires, entry into the belly of the monster, the bedlam of erotic orgies, and, in myths of future catastrophe, the expectation of plagues, cosmic conflagration, wars—all of these symbols represent regression into chaos; they symbolize the chaos that is universally accepted as the womb of the new creation.

In Eliade's terminology the family of related symbols for chaos is referred to simply as the "symbolism of chaos." Here "symbolism" is understood to imply a system of religious meaning capable of guiding our interpretation of innumerable particular hierophanies or revelations of the sacred, of reality, of being. The hermeneutical value of the symbolism of chaos lies in leading us, when we discern a related symbolic manifestation, to its basically optimistic meaning as abolition of the past and passage to life. It is obvious that there is also a cluster of symbols that comprise the symbolism of creation, of new life, of cosmogony.

Symbolic thinking, Eliade goes on to say, is not the exclusive possession of the child or the poet or the insane; it is an innate mode of human cognition that "comes before language and discursive reason. The symbol reveals certain aspects of reality—the deepest aspects—which defy any other means of knowledge."[14] Thus they are clearly not "irresponsible creations of the psyche; they respond to a need and fulfil a function, that of bringing to light the most hidden modalities of being."[15]

Images and symbols are by their very structure *multi-valent*, revealing an array of meanings all of which are true. For any one human discipline to feel that its concern has exhausted the meaning of a symbol is not only unduly restrictive and arbitrary but also for Eliade patently false. Images and symbols yield therefore a system of meaning that must finally open out upon the transcendent, and thus ultimately they imitate or represent the Image or exemplary model itself. "To have imagination," Eliade contends, "is to be able to see the world in its totality, for the power and the mission of the Images is to *show* all that remains refractory to the concept."[16]

The myth, Eliade concludes, "as well as the symbols it brings into play, never quite disappears from the present world of the psyche; it only changes its aspect and disguises its operations."[17] Symbols come from such depths in man that "it is impossible that they should not be found again in any and every existential situation of man in the Cosmos."[18] Thus we can readily understand the concern of many literary critics for a dimension beyond the literal. For if one accepts Eliade's thesis, he must be open to the fact that the author is almost certainly not aware of all of the implications of his work; there is room for archaic symbols to reappear even in realist or naturalist writers. Significant, too, for our examination of contemporary repetitions of apocalyptic symbols is Eliade's suggestion that spiritual renewal may hopefully come for modern man from the rediscovery of the meaning of faded symbols.[19]

II

Both Judaism and Christianity developed myths of future catastrophe, of an end that would come only once in the history of the world. The apocalyptic literature that appeared late in Judaism reached its perfection in the last book of the Christian canon. The end will come only once because, in the Judaeo-Christian world-view, time is linear and irreversible. Not that there are not suggestions of the cyclic in the pattern of its liturgy and in the "return to innocence" that is implicit in the *metanoia* urged upon the individual; these analogies to primitive cult are indeed there. But time is not cyclic, and this is the uniqueness of Judaeo-Christianity in the perspective of world religions. It has accepted the irreversibility of time, the terror of history. It sees the value of the historical hour for salvation. Moreover, since the Incarnation of Christ took place in history, history has shown itself capable of sustaining hierophany in a much more profound sense even than God's revelation of himself to the Hebrew people in the events of the covenant. In the Incarnation, according to Christian belief, God himself became event for man in history. So any Judaeo-Christian expectation of an end to the world would obviously have to come *in* history, even if it would mean the end of time and of history.

According to R. H. Charles, Hebrew apocalypse made a substantial contribution to the religious thought of Israel, and so to the religious thought of man. And in so doing it advanced considerably beyond the richest thought of the prophets of Israel. It professed belief, in its maturest form, in a catastrophic end to the present world, with the expectation of a "new heaven and a new earth" as the work of God extended beyond the fold of Israel to all men as individuals, whereas the noblest expectation of the prophets had confined itself to Israel as a nation.[20] And, in both Judaism and Christianity, there is belief that the end of the world will be preceded by a series of cosmic and historical calamities that will act as its announcement—famines, droughts, wars, the appearance of the Antichrist, celestial signs, and so forth. Eliade puts these signs preceding the end in mythical perspective by pointing out that they are evidence of "the traditional motif of extreme decadence, of the triumph of evil and darkness, which precede the change of aeon and the renewal of the cosmos."

The most significant aspect of Old Testament apocalypse, though, would seem to be in the area of its unlimited view of history, its acceptance of the totality of history as it had accepted the totality of the human race. And thus it distinguished itself again from even the best of the prophetic literature. Prophecy dealt only incidentally with the past, concerned as it was with the present and the future and the organic relationship between the two; whereas apocalypse strove to show how past, present, and future were woven together into a single unity. Apocalyptic literature was interested in the future as the solution to the past and the present; but it also sought, in Charles's words, "to get behind the surface and penetrate to the essence of events, the spiritual purposes and forces that underlie and give them their real significance. With this end in view apocalyptic sketched in outline the history of the world and of mankind, the origin of evil, its course, and inevitable overthrow, the ultimate triumph of righteousness, and the final consummation of all things."[22] The total view of history hopefully affords sufficient distance from the crisis at hand to permit the believer to discover God's will for the present as well as the overall meaning of human existence.[23]

There are two eminent commentators on Israel's apocalyptic tradition whose interpretation is so divergent
from the one taken here that they must certainly be
heard; they are Gerhard von Rad and Martin Buber. It
is precisely because of the general nature of the overview
of history sketched above that von Rad faults Hebrew
apocalypse for being "devoid of theology."[24] It knows
nothing, he asserts, of those saving acts of God in history
that the theology of the prophets was rooted in. Von
Rad, moreover, agrees with Martin Buber about the
determinism of Old Testament apocalypse. Its eschatological and transcendental dualism, von Rad claims,
clearly differentiates between the present and the future
aeon; and the future is "already pre-existent in the
world above and come[s] down from there to earth."[25]
Martin Buber focuses on the predictive content of apocalypse and sees the clear resolution of the conflict
between good and evil in God's favor as an indication of
the radical determinism of apocalyptic writing. His
thesis is that prophecy, on the other hand, is open-ended
concerning the historical hour; its structure is basically
dialogical, with God and man working out together the
future of the world. Yet even though he admits that the
faith inherent in prophecy is the same as for apocalypse,
namely, that God will prevail, he insists that prophecy
as an expression of the achievement of the human spirit
in its relationship with transcendence preserves more
tellingly man's freedom insofar as it emphasizes man's
capacity to turn either toward or away from God.

Apocalypse, says Buber, overlooks history and man's
capacity for shaping it in favor of the consummation to

be received from outside of history: "The mature apoc-alyptic, moreover, no longer knows an historical future in the real sense. The end of all history is near. . . . The proper and paradoxical subject of the late apocalyptic is a future that is no longer in time, and he anticipates this consummation so that for him all that may yet come in history no longer has an historical character. Man can-not achieve this future, but he also has nothing more to achieve."[26] On the other hand, Buber continues, proph-ecy does not fix the future because its understanding of the transcendent is of a God who wants man to turn to him with full freedom out of his hopelessness. Buber insists that this is the prophetic *theologem*, although he admits that it is "never expressed as such but firmly embedded in the foundations of Hebrew prophecy."[27]

Taking an overall view of his treatment of the distinc-tion between prophecy and apocalypse, one wishes that Buber had been as generous in selecting material from apocalypse as he was in determining the nature of proph-ecy. He has, for example, simply ignored all of Messianic prophecy and the content of its inspired word—which gets to be quite specific, almost deterministic, as far as the nation is concerned—in favor of the dialogical reci-procity that he finds in Jeremiah's debate with God. In *Pointing the Way*, he concentrates upon the Fourth Book of Ezra for his analysis of the meaning of apoc-alypse. His scholarly concern does not extend to the New Testament Book of Revelation, where a dialogical framework is indeed implicit in the letters to the churches. Moreover, the Book of Revelation is aware of God's saving act in Jesus; this is actually its pervasive concern. Von Rad's argument, therefore, about the lack of theological perspective in Old Testament apocalypse obviously could not be leveled against the Book of Revelation. And, as William Beardslee observes, the determinism of apocalyptic literature, "as in Calvinism, is an expression of wonder at the glory of God."[28] The present crisis is so distressing that the believer knows he can be saved only by God. Buber and von Rad notwithstanding, it is certainly a respectable scholarly approach to the relationship between prophecy and apocalypse to see them not as diametrically opposed, with apocalypse representing the disintegration of a tradition, but rather, following Charles and other standard commentators, as stages in a developing understanding of faith.

Few modern commentators on the literature of apocalypse, specifically on its most developed expression in the New Testament, will stress or even mention what Buber and von Rad object to as the other-worldly aspect of apocalyptic literature, of a consummation coming from God outside of history. N. Turner, for example, in *Peake's Commentary on the Bible*, says that the Book of Revelation is "much more concerned with the course of world-history than with the fate of souls after death."[29] H. H. Rowley sees Revelation as having at least this in common with the rest of apocalyptic literature, that it expresses faith in a God who is directing the course of human history according to a plan that he intends to see through to completion; and this decidedly includes his victory over evil.[30] Andre Feuillet, a Catholic commentator, feels that Revelation gives a Christian meaning to history by inveighing against the easy opti-

mism of imminent victory; and in presenting life as an
enduring struggle that will eventually be won by Christ,
Revelation offers us a "theological datum" rather than
a chronological observation. Feuillet, considering the
theological implications of the titles attributed to Jesus,
judges the book to possess one of the most developed
Christologies of the New Testament. Like the Epistle
to the Hebrews, he notes, it counsels perseverance amid
stress. In relation to the Old Testament, and thus to
the expanded interest in human history that Charles
noted, Revelation shows how the true meaning of history, going all the way back to Genesis, becomes clear
only in Christ.[31]

If apocalypse is not primarily concerned with another
world, what is it concerned with? An attempt to rede-
fine apocalypse could obviously appear to be just another
word game, or an evasion of what everyone accepts as
true. For even though Turner can insist that the apocalyptic style developed "in periods of stress to encourage
readers to persevere in faith and good works,"[32] a tradi-
tionalist understanding would jump immediately to the
conclusion that the obvious reason why Christians are
to persevere under trial is that their true home is not
really of this world.

I suggest that the import of apocalypse as it developed
in the Hebrew and Christian canons had nothing to do
with holding the carrot of eternity before the believer's
nose. It is true that history is seen as a mystery of God's
planning, a mystery that will ultimately be revealed as
his victory over the perversity of human freedom; but
the precise *raison d'être* for apocalypse is to deny the

imminence of easy victory, to force Jews and Christians alike to accept the agony of history, the birth-pangs of creation. My emphasis here on the theme of denial of imminent victory does not derogate from the obvious apocalyptic concentration on the end. The desire for "total presence" that Beardslee sees embodied in apocalyptic form is necessitated paradoxically, as he notes, by "the threat of a total victory of evil."[33] Feuillet proposes that the basic teaching of Revelation, a viewpoint common to the whole New Testament, is that "Christians are now assisting at the painful but guaranteed birth-pangs of the definitive era of final salvation."[34] Elsewhere Feuillet writes: "The Apocalypse does not at all seek to soothe its readers by dulling illusions of peace; rather, the author shows the life of the Church as endlessly plagued by terrible crimes of every kind, bringing thereby a needed counterbalance to the naive and unjustified self-deception that progress is automatic and imminent for the Church."[35]

The rejection of naive optimism and the denial of imminent victory is the message confirmed by the very structure of the Book of Revelation, and this type of consideration is obviously germane to our analysis of literary apocalypse. Its progressively expanding rhythm of sevens, each of which creates the illusion of a complete vision only to explode into a subsequent vision of seven, continually shatters the mood of expectation that the author seemed so carefully to be creating. Each of the six weeks of seven days, as Austin Farrer has demonstrated so capably, each successive series of visions, is intended to create and shatter the illusion of imminent completion of the apocalypse.[36] Thus, the total effect of the ever-retreating horizon of fulfillment is to support a mood of genuine hope amid frustration.

The place of Revelation in the New Testament canon, obviously crucial for understanding its meaning, is analogous to the position of apocalyptic literature in the Old Testament. For the development of apocalypse late in the Old Testament period was undoubtedly a response to unfulfilled prophecy, just as Revelation marked faith's rejection of the illusion of imminent surcease that had been created by the advent of the Messiah (an illusion that is very much in evidence in the earlier New Testament writings). The closer man comes to God, the more tangible his revelation, the greater the human temptation to expect immediate deliverance from the terror of existence. Revelation, therefore, represents the most mature reflection of the New Testament faith. Expressed in poetic language, though, it has often eluded the grasp of a church plagued by the logic of scholasticism.

Apocalypse is a response to cultural crisis. It grows out of that sense of loss that results from the passing of an old world-view. Of all of the recent analysts of apocalypse, no one has expressed this more precisely than Amos Wilder:

> Common to all true apocalyptic is a situation characterized by anomie, a loss of "world," or erosion of structures, psychic and cultural, with the consequent nakedness to Being or immediacy to the Mystery. Hence the rhetorics of this "panic" exposure in which existence itself is at stake, involving antinomies of life and death, light and darkness, knowledge and nescience, order and chaos. And it can never be only a question

of the individual. It is a juncture which renews the archaic crisis of all existence, that of survival, the viability of life, the viability of the human. Since inherited structures and mediacies of a dependable order are forfeit, the only available dramatizations of the crisis and of any projected "future" will necessarily have a pre-cultural character. Pre-cultural, first in a temporal sense: a return to archaic motifs and to deeply buried hierophanies of the community. But pre-cultural also in the sense of a language responsive to the unmediated dynamics that underlie all Being and Becoming.[37]

In the Book of Revelation, loss of world takes the form of the imagined darkness attendant upon the rejected expectation of an imminent establishment of God's final kingdom; mature faith accepts the enduring struggle that historical existence entails. In contemporary literature, loss of world expresses itself in the same arcane images, the pre-cultural images of conflict and destruction that Amos Wilder describes, yet frequently without the sense of continuity that existed through the period of normative Christian apocalypse. One obvious reason for this would seem to be the loss of faith that allows one to project a future. Cultural turmoil is reflected in the breakdown of the language tradition that holds together man's view of the world; yet throughout the agonizing passage to another linguistic expression of faith, the reality of faith must apparently remain, though inarticulate, if man is to bridge the cultural chasm with hope.

Apocalypse, of all the New Testament literary forms, expresses clear awareness of man's painful "fall into history,"[38] a phrase of Mircea Eliade's that captures perfectly the realization underlying apocalyptic vision. The full implication of living in history, of the ravages of conditioned human existence, is what is intended by this expression. The very place of salvation is now an obstacle to salvation. The very event in which God comes to man must be sought in the obscurity of history. When the sacred manifested itself only in the cosmos, it was fairly easy to recognize, particularly when an object was charged with power or when through the repetition of a ritual sacred time began again. The Christian, though, "has continually to *choose*, to try to distinguish, in the tangle of historical events, the event which, *for him*, may be charged with a saving significance."[39] The day-to-day agony of discernment is the result of Christian acceptance of the fall into history, and it is this realization that the display of violent images in Revelation gives witness to. Christians thus spare themselves at least the futile agony of discerning the end. They accept, and even yearn for, the end as fulfillment of a promise, God's promise of fidelity, but in the meantime turn their full attention to the ambiguous face of history.

A clear purpose of the Book of Revelation, then, is to aid the experience of mature faith, the acceptance of a call to work out one's salvation in the ambiguity of irreversible time. Final salvation is not at hand; in fact, the experience of faith is an acceptance of hope that makes no demands. One cannot escape history by thinking that the work is over or that it will be ended shortly. If one expects an imminent end, Revelation teaches, his hope is indeed vain—and his faith patently immature.

Although there is certainly no need to enter into the debate about the author of Revelation, whether he was

John the apostle or some other well-known John, I must nonetheless point out that the continuing dispute over authorship opens up the possibility that the New Testament apocalypse was written pseudonymously as all Jewish apocalypses after 200 B.C. undoubtedly were— and of necessity, as R. H. Charles has shown.[40] Apocalypse in the Old Testament dates from the period in Judaism when the law was everything, and the only way the writers could proclaim their very urgent message concerning the genuine eschatological thrust of their faith over the din of legalism was to give their work the sanctity of tradition. The author of Revelation perhaps chose the name of one of the sons of thunder because he wanted that association to add weight to his words of judgment against those who would codify their faith in Christ into easy optimism. John had asked to share the chalice and did no doubt in a measure beyond his expectation, and, says the author of Revelation, so would anyone who calls himself a follower of Christ.

The very medium of Christian faith *is* hope, Jürgen Moltmann has reminded us: "The eschatological is not one element *of* Christianity, but it is the medium of Christian faith as such, the key in which everything in it is set, the glow that suffuses everything here in the dawn of an expected new day."[41] It is a medium though without historical specification, without perhaps any other content than the one demonstrated by the author of Revelation; namely that God *will* fulfill his promises. The emphasis in Revelation is on the future, but in such a way that belief in the fulfillment of the promise can enlighten one's acceptance of the past and strengthen his approach to the present. Hope alone can illumine the future.

Apocalyptic literature, moreover, uses the mythic framework of the regeneration of the world as a macro-cosmic idiom for another important Christian concern, the *metanoia* of the individual. The author of Revelation is certainly conscious of the fact that he addresses the individual hearer within the context of his church. "Hear, you who have ears to hear, what the Spirit says to the Churches!"[42] Christian *metanoia* is always a turning toward God by turning to the neighbor; so when we speak of the regeneration of the individual, our frame of theological reference is not merely vertical. The regeneration that is promised to the world is offered to the hearer now if he will turn from his former evil ways and accept as reality the possibility of starting anew in response to the word spoken to him. Judgment is leveled against the churches within the imaginative context of cosmic judgment, and the norm that is offered in support of judgment is the expected righteousness of Christ. Thus the imagery of conflict found in Revelation sharpens the call to repentance, most specifically for the sin of presumption.

The image of the eternal city which concludes the vision of Revelation is a perfect complement to the para-disiacal myth of Genesis. Men fail in righteousness when they turn away from the daily agony of building up the city of man. The myth of paradise, naive and primitive as a statement of man's origin, becomes reasonable escha-

tological expectation at the end of the Book of Revelation, a more mature expression of religious belief when
viewed as the destiny man gropes toward in the darkness
of the future. The exemplary pattern of behavior is no
longer what the gods did *in illo tempore,* but the promised city of light and love that Christians are in agony
to bring forth.

A pattern has been developing in this exposition of
the primitive and Judaeo-Christian usage of apocalypse
that can hopefully be stated explicitly at this point. I
suggest that the elements that are normative for traditional or classical apocalypse are judgment, catastrophe,
and renewal. Judgment is leveled against man, a judgment that is couched in the dramatic language of conflict and catastrophe, threatened or realized or both. The
purpose of the conjunction of judgment and catastrophe is the same one that prompted the primitive return
to chaos and the Judaeo-Christian testamentary conclusion with apocalypse: renewal, *metanoia,* new life, but
within the context of mature, creative hope. Among
the primitives the norm for judging was the pattern
of the gods' behavior, preserved from the beginning.
The Judaeo-Christian norm is eschatological expectation, the projected vision of faith. Primitive religion
therefore renews the present on the basis of the past,
whereas Judaeo-Christian hope is based on the expectation of future fulfillment. The former conception of
time is clearly cyclic and closed, the latter linear and
open. This essay at definition will hopefully emerge with
even greater clarity as we proceed to an investigation of
the evidence for apocalypse in the American experience.

III

In the title essay of his *Errand into the Wilderness*, Perry Miller suggests that the Puritans by the second and third generations had taken a rather dim view of their mission of reformation.[43] Their errand into the wilderness had two purposes, as Miller sees it, and in both instances it failed. The Puritans were presumptuous enough to think they could redeem England and Europe by example; yet the "city upon a hill"[44] for all Europe to see never materialized. And if the colonists concentrated simply on their errand as a mission from God—a covenant to be faithful to—they had little to be proud of because sin still seemed to get more than an ordinary nod.

As evidence of apocalypse in their theological writings, Miller points to the emphasis on declension and apostasy in Puritan exhortations to renewal as early as 1660. Sermons on imminent judgment and the visitation of God's wrath were charged with fire and brimstone. Miller's contention is that the rhetoric of sin was little more than a ritual incantation that barely disguised their admission of failure at reformation. This token payment on their obligations to their covenant, says Miller, freed them for the far more lucrative secular enterprise of exploiting the wilderness. He concludes: "Under the guise of this mounting wail of sinfulness, this incessant and never successful cry for repentance, the Puritans launched themselves upon the process of Americanization."[45]

Despite Perry Miller's preeminent position as the dean of American Puritan studies, it is undoubtedly safe to

say that his interpretation of the second and third gen-
eration jeremiads as shields of a spreading secularization
is anachronistic. America has developed apace with the
modernization of the Western world; the nineteenth
century is, therefore, a more reasonable period to ascribe
the beginnings of secularization to. Scholars of American Puritanism have, in the past decade, faulted Miller
on a number of points. The idea of declension is, in
Michael McGiffert's words, "too simple a category for
the complex changes which Miller traced."[46] For the most
part, Miller's critics deny the coherent pattern to Puritan thought that Miller discusses under the monolithic
rubric of the "New England mind." Recent scholarship
demonstrates the pluralism in Puritan writings; and
especially in the matter of Puritan theology, it stresses
the importance of the New England "heart." "This
emphasis on Puritan emotionality is reinforced," Mc-
Giffert states, "by scholars who have called attention to
the Puritans' expectation of the imminent Eschaton. . . .
Spiritual fervor was undoubtedly intensified by the chiliasm of New Englanders who beyond their desire to conduct a reformist flank-attack on old England—beyond
all considerations of earthly consequence whatever—
regarded their new world as the beginning of the
world's end."[47]

The hopes of the men who came to Massachusetts Bay
and Plymouth were spawned by an age of apocalyptic
expectation. Luther's second preface to the Book of
Revelation in 1545 had returned to the time-honored
historical interpretation of the prophetic element in the
work. The events described in visions and symbols were

historical, he reminded his reader; Christendom needed only to decipher the mysterious message. In Luther's interpretation the millennium of peace prophesied in chapter 20 had already passed into history with the first thousand years of Christianity; they were living then in the period of the last loosing of Satan, typified by the sins of the papacy.[48] It was therefore characteristic of the preaching of the Reformation and the following century to consider the last days described in Revelation as already in progress. H. Richard Niebuhr sketches the temper of the times in these words: "Not only impatient expectation but also the sense of a crisis in time made the coming kingdom seem very real and near. All around there were signs that the old order of life was passing; an ominous sense of catastrophe and an invigorating promise of newness of life were conveyed by the rumors of battles, of Roman decadence, of new worlds discovered, of novel ideas and inventions."[49]

It is likewise anachronistic to interpret the Puritan expectation of the Eschaton in anything other than the traditional terms of salvation for the individual and the spiritual consummation of eternity. Niebuhr warns against reading the Puritans and expecting to find there "the utopian note of nineteenth century romanticism or twentieth century idealism."[50] From Michael Wigglesworth's *The Day of Doom*, the "first best seller in the annals of the American book trade,"[51] through Jonathan Edwards' "Sinners in the Hands of an Angry God," the emphasis is on the judgment of the individual and on an otherworldly reward or punishment.

There were, however, differences of emphasis during

the seventeenth and eighteenth centuries. When Puritans thought of the kingdom of God, "it was not a society of peace and concord to be established by men of good will; it was rather the living reality of God's present rule."[52] For the Puritans, "the goal of life was eternity rather than a new time, immortality of the spirit rather than resurrection of the body."[53] The concern for individual salvation led them to conceive of society in rather static terms; there was no destiny for the community comparable to the promise held out to the human soul. In the eighteenth century, the Great Awakening announced the advent of Christ's reign in men's hearts. Thus, when theologians imagined the promise of the kingdom of Christ, "they did not think in the first place of a warless world wherein lions and lambs would lie down together, . . . they thought rather of the cleansing of the inward parts, of the restoration to man of inner harmony, and of the elimination of the war in the members, whence all other wars and fighting came."[54] For the revivalists, "the coming kingdom meant crisis as well as promise."[55] There would be judgment first, and only then the new world of God.

The nineteenth century—that time of great hopefulness stretching from the Revolution to the World War —is characterized by Niebuhr as "the period of the coming kingdom."[56] As the decades rolled by, optimism concerning the anticipated Christian revolution in history began to supplement the two centuries of concern for the promise of the heavenly city. There had nevertheless been a foreshadowing of this developing interest in the kingdom on earth. The Quakers believed not only in "a manifestation of divine majesty and the apocalypse of human sin" but also and even more in "the reign of love."[57] Love would spread among men with the growing experience of the kingdom of Christ. The Great Awakening, by emphasizing the effects of Christ's kingdom in men's hearts, also contributed to the American tendency toward millenarian expectation. Yet while American Christians began to think of promise in social terms, the human unit remained paradoxically the individual, and so crisis was still conceived "in terms of death."[58] This propensity of the apocalyptic imagination to focus on the death of the individual has had a marked effect upon the literary mind, as we will note later, particularly in chapter 3.

The hope of a radical transformation of earthly life did not obliterate the expectation of heavenly bliss; it did, however, become the prey of many exaggerations. Hope "was secularized by being detached from its context of faith in the sovereignty [of God] and of the experience of grace, while it was attached to the ideas of human sovereignty and natural freedom. It was nationalized, being used to support the feeling of national superiority and of manifest destiny. It was confused with the progress of industrialism and capitalism."[59] The ultimate note of the nationalization of the kingdom was sounded by the growing American belief in divine favoritism. Niebuhr expresses it this way: "The old idea of American Christians as a chosen people who had been called to a special task was turned into the notion of a chosen nation especially favored."[60] Despite the secularization of the millenarian movement, it is unquestionably true that the Christian experience "was one of its major sources."[61] The naive optimism of nineteenth century liberalism was "rooted in the Christian gospel."[62]

The death of the individual, so important a theme in popular preaching, offered no problems to the imagination of the theologian. During the first centuries of the American experience, however, the advances in science did leave theologians groping in the dark for reasonable explanations of the end of the world and the final judgment. Wigglesworth, who was more a poet than a theologian, if indeed he was either, was still operating in the medieval tradition of a highly specific schedule of the last days, which was actually nothing more than a literal reading of Revelation with a few scattered patches over the discrepancies. Yet in his verse apocalypse he failed to commit himself about whether the end would mean annihilation or transformation of the physical earth.[63] Natural scientists were already claiming that the world was indestructible.

Thomas Burnet proposed in 1681 that the providence of God and natural causality could coincide in such a way that greater proximity to the sun, for example, would cause the earth to ignite. Only six years later Newton demonstrated the rigid laws of universal motion, and Burnet's noble attempt to save faith in literal apocalypse collapsed. Cotton Mather, however, pointed out what should have been obvious: If God had established the law of gravity, he could certainly interrupt it. William Whiston's new theory of the earth in 1696, just fifteen years after Burnet ended the world to leave only heaven, called for catastrophe by comets, which would be all the needed purgation before a secular millennium. But perhaps Jonathan Edwards was the wisest of all; the man whom Miller calls "the greatest artist of the apocalypse"[64] avoided a mechanical explanation of the last judgment altogether, apparently giving up any thought of scaring men into virtue, thus taking a welcome step toward a less literal understanding of apocalypse.

America had no prehistory, at least that the white settlers knew or cared about, and so it was only natural that its preoccupation should be with the future. American Protestants believed, as we have already seen, that they were part of the end-time. Yet, by the nineteenth century, the future of faith was undergoing a severe struggle for survival against the inroads of science and liberalism. The first three centuries of American preoccupation with apocalypse end with a process of secularization well under way. The cult of nature was capturing the American mind, and manifest destiny assumed the dignity of religious belief. The land and the natives were exploited; success easily attained aggravated American need for achievement. And so in keeping with the tenor of the times in Western society, and adequately bolstered by advances in the study of evolution, a myth of unlimited progress developed that would become the background for the literary rebirth of genuine apocalypse. Perry Miller describes this secular chiliasm:

> Thus the nineteenth century was completing the seventeenth's errand into the wilderness: the meaning was at last emerging, the meaning hidden from Winthrop and from the Puritan pioneers. After all, it now appeared, they had been dispatched

into the forests not to set up a holy city on some Old World
model but to commence the gigantic industrial expansion
which, launched upon a limitless prospect, would demonstrate
the folly of anxieties about, or even of a lust for, the end of
this physical universe. . . . If monomania it was, then out
of it the American nineteenth century proclaimed that the
meaning of America's errand into the wilderness had disclosed
itself as an errand without an end.[65]

A distinctively literary strand of American apocalypse developed during the nineteenth century; the
creators of the apocalyptic trend were novelists, not
theologians. Harry Levin, treating Hawthorne, Poe, and
Melville in *The Power of Blackness*, exposes the dark
side of the nineteenth-century literary imagination as opposed to the official optimism: "Where the voice of the
majority is by definition affirmative, the spirit of independence is likeliest to manifest itself by employing the
negative: by saying *no* in thunder—as Melville wrote to
Hawthorne—though bidden by the devil himself to say
yes."[66] And although Levin makes no attempt to situate
his analysis of "blackness" in a broader literary landscape, his reading of their works supports this interpretation of the place of apocalypse in American literature.
Genuine apocalypse had always functioned as a warning against the presumption of man.

Thus the literary phase of American apocalypse that
develops with the maturation of our national literature,
from the middle of the nineteenth century to the present, reflects a strong reaction against the easy optimism
of the late nineteenth and early twentieth centuries and
later a poignant response to the succession of global hot

and cold wars. It reflects as well the process of secularization that began in the nineteenth century and blos-
somed into the anomie of the century of unrestrained
technology. My principal task in subsequent chapters
will be the analysis of certain representative works in
this literary apocalyptic tradition. Thus far I have
treated the three constitutive elements of traditional
apocalypse only within their historical contexts. Catastrophe, judgment, and renewal must now be refined
from the vantage point of symbolism as a basis for the
critical analysis of individual works. Each of these clus-
ters of symbols can be specified as primitive, Judaeo-
Christian, and also tentatively as secular. The term
"secular apocalypse" will be used here simply to denote
the use of the worldly analogue for the traditional
religious symbolism.

IV

Catastrophe as symbolism can be distinguished initially
into signs of warning and the imagination of the end
itself. In the symbolism of apocalypse concerned with
the warning signs of impending disaster, the appearance
of the man of iniquity, the Antichrist, is an expectation
preceding the end that goes back to one of the earliest
Christian writings, Paul's Second Letter to the Thessa-
lonians. Where the explicit image of Satan is used, this
symbolism can be understood as Christian in imagination, if not necessarily in intention. The symbolism of
warning may be either microcosmic or macrocosmic
depending upon the range of the felt presence of evil.

More often than not, the tone of the work will indicate that, even where the presence of evil is limited apparently to the ambience of an individual's life, the apocalyptic consequences are to be read on a grander scale because the individual is also somehow typical.

As the secular image of the last loosing of Satan, we can anticipate the presentation of the superpromiser whose protean face reflects the evil of the society he woos. R. W. B. Lewis traces this strand of "ludicrous catastrophe"[67] in American literature from Melville's *The Confidence-Man*, through Twain's *The Mysterious Stranger* and West's *The Day of the Locust*, into the present in Ellison, Barth, Pynchon, and Heller.[68]

That the times immediately preceding the end are characterized by a general breakdown of moral standards, which explains the presence and acceptability of Satan in his many disguises, is a symbolism that is common also to cyclic myths of catastrophe. In *kali yuga*, known as the "evil age," the last of the four ages of the Indian cosmic cycle, only a quarter of the moral order remains. Man and society here reach the extreme point of moral disintegration. The catalogue of evil found in the *Vishnu Purana* could readily serve as the imaginative framework for the antigospel of the confidence man. Mircea Eliade sums up the moral chaos of the *kali yuga* in this way:

> It is the only age in which property alone confers social rank; wealth becomes the only motive of the virtues, passion and lust the only bonds between the married, falsehood and deception the first condition of success in life, sexuality the sole means of enjoyment, while external, merely ritualistic

religion is confused with spirituality. For several thousand years, be it understood, we have been living in *kali yuga*.[69]

The other aspect of the symbolism of catastrophe focuses on "the end" itself—if not of all mankind, at least of a phase of its social history. The death of the individual as typical of a phase of society or of the fate await-ing a certain unacceptable response to living is another significant motif in this vein of the tradition. Thus, as in our description of the symbolism of warning, the imagination of the end may also be microcosmic as well as macrocosmic. The extension of catastrophe, however, would seem to matter little as far as the essence of apocalypse is concerned.

It is more difficult here than in the preceding discussion of warning signs to discern differences between the primitive and Judaeo-Christian imaginations without entering into a consideration of their respective attitudes toward time and history. Generally speaking, therefore, the primitive imagination of the end will be expressed in images related to chaos, but a chaos that is not of its nature final. Thus darkness is an ideal archaic symbol of chaos because it is regularly associated with the light to which it ultimately yields. Customary natural turbulence, such as an earthquake, storm or flood, is also an appropriate primitive symbol of catastrophe.

Water and fire are the two principal Judaeo-Christian symbols of cosmic catastrophe. Chapter 3 of the Second Letter of Peter establishes fire as the specific mode of the earth's final dissolution, corresponding to its first destruction by water as preserved in the Genesis legend.

The power of water to cleanse and purify makes it an obvious instrument of judgment. The relationship between fire and purity is perhaps not as clear. Gaston Bachelard considers three instances of the use of fire that support its appropriateness as a symbol of purification.[70] Fire suppresses nauseous odors and arrests putrefaction; hence cooked food is considered purer to eat. The refiner's fire reduces metal to its purest state. And in agriculture fire is used to destroy weeds and purify the soil. But most important of all, perhaps, is fire's association with light, making it an ideal symbol of the purifying passage to new life.[71] Moreover, in developed Judaeo-Christian apocalypse, catastrophe is a *once for all* occurrence; hence we expect either death or universal destruction.

In the secular imagination, cataclysm—if it is conceived at all—is predictably refracted into some sign of civil or international conflict such as riots, war, or nuclear devastation, where the evil is unequivocally man-made. The cataclysm may or may not be final. Where a millenarian viewpoint is secularized, history may be imagined—as we have already indicated—as a process of transformation without end.

In speaking of the symbolism of judgment, I refer to images that represent a mythic norm of judgment against which the action of the novel and its characters are read. In the ritual return to chaos of primitive man, the norm of judgment is the pattern of the gods enacted in the ritual. To refer back to the beginning, the time of the gods, is equivalent to preserving the memory of the original innocence of the race. Thus, the imagery of paradise with its emphasis on man's origins contributes to this primitive symbolism of judgment. The Judaeo-Christian norm of judgment is the coming Messianic kingdom, the Heavenly Jerusalem. Its image of the perfect man and his society comes from the future rather than the past. The secular symbolism of judgment will have to be derived from the works themselves selected for analysis. More often than not, the general norm against which man is judged worthy of destruction or capable of indefinite progress is a view of human nature that from a Christian point of view would be considered heretical. It makes sense after all to assume that the reason the secular mind envisions catastrophe or progress without end is that in interpreting man and his situation in history it has either lost hope in the future of man or lost faith in the promise of God.

The symbolism of new life is a simple derivative of judgment and the imagination's grasp of time. Newness in the primitive imagination is scarcely more than a fresh start at something which has already repeatedly been begun; it is ultimately a repetition of the beginning since time is cyclic. For the Judaeo-Christian imagination, renewal means not just beginning again but actual growth or development. What is new is genuinely new because time is irreversible. The secular imagination either provides for nothing new because its despair is final or projects a simple continuation of history because its presumption is total. We will call the former the apocalypse of despair, the latter presumptive eschatology —and thus remove it from the scope of our concern. The nineteenth century was tending toward an anti-apocalyptic understanding of history; for the ultimate ideal of transformation without suffering—of progress without end—is a denial of the basic structure of apocalypse. As a world-view it may be understandable eschatology, but not apocalypse. Cataclysm is the necessary apocalyptic passage to new life.

A key apocalyptic symbol is the number seven, and where it is used we will have to take special note of its relation to the treatment of time. Seven represents completion or perfection insofar as it has been taken traditionally as a temporal unit of completed measurement, the week. We noted earlier how the author of Revelation employs the structural basis of successive sevens to destroy the illusion of an imminent Parousia. Use of seven as a symbolic structure is ample indication of apocalyptic purpose. Where a basic pattern of seven yields an eighth unit, the beginning of a new week, for example, the view of time is clearly open-ended, respecting the possibility of new life. But where seven is an enclosed structural pattern, we will almost definitely be dealing with the secular view of apocalypse in which catastrophe is final.

Thus far we have considered the various types of symbolism that will be indicative of apocalypse in the works awaiting our analysis. A novel is normally considered apocalyptic if, within these general structures, it possesses at least two of the specific symbolisms of apocalypse: catastrophe and judgment. R. W. B. Lewis has pointed out that modern authors can almost all be distinguished according to the nature and causes of the cataclysm they describe.[72] But it should be clear already that the symbolism of catastrophe, expected or realized or both, and the symbolism of judgment together do not comprise the totality of normative apocalypse. All primitive myths of catastrophe as well as the Judaeo-Christian apocalypses result in something new; they are basically optimistic in that they yield new life, a new creation. Literature, therefore, that omits symbolism of re-creation as an integral part of its aesthetic structure is obviously not traditional, although it may certainly be considered apocalyptic. We have tentatively called it apocalypse of despair. What distinguishes the Judaeo-Christian from the primitive, as we have seen, is the treatment of time and the source of hope. Time for the former is truly linear, for the latter merely cyclic. The primitive imagination depends upon the remembrance of origins, the Judaeo-Christian on eschatological expectation.

What remains to be done is the major task of describing some of the American literary variations on the apocalyptic form. Obviously, no attempt will be made at an exhaustive survey of the field; a selection has been made of certain representative novels that are generally considered to contain apocalyptic elements. A few titles were selected because they represent less well-known but nonetheless important works of major authors. For example, no more apocalyptic novel has appeared in the history of American literature than *Moby-Dick*. Yet in treating Melville I have chosen instead *The Confidence-Man*, which has been receiving greater critical attention in the last two decades but which obviously has neither the reputation nor the scope of his masterpiece. The twelve novels taken together will, I hope, contribute to the understanding of the use of apocalyptic symbolism in the American novel.

Chapter 2 is devoted to the works of Hawthorne, Melville, and Twain, respectively: *The Blithedale Romance, The Confidence-Man,* and *The Mysterious Stranger.* Together they will afford enlightening comparative insights into the apocalyptic imagination of three of our greatest writers of fiction of the nineteenth century. In chapter 3 we move firmly into the twentieth century, considering Faulkner's *As I Lay Dying,* Nathanael West's *Miss Lonelyhearts,* and Flannery O'Connor's *The Violent Bear It Away.* None of these works has the cosmic dimension of nineteenth-century or contemporary apocalypse; nevertheless they employ an intensity and often subtlety of imagery that neither went before nor has followed. The selected novels come from writers with Protestant, Jewish, and Roman Catholic backgrounds. Chapter 4 attempts to analyze the spectrum of the Afro-American apocalyptic imagination. For cultural reasons that are obvious to anyone who has lived in the United States during the last quarter century, apocalyse has been very much in the minds of our best black writers. The titles are from Ralph Ellison, James Baldwin, and Richard Wright—*Invisible Man, Go Tell It on the Mountain,* and *Native Son,* respectively. Finally, in chapter 5 I will investigate three contemporary contributions to the strand of humorous apocalypse that R. W. B. Lewis has explored in his essay "Days of Wrath and Laughter." These last novels to be analyzed are John Barth's *The End of the Road,* Thomas Pynchon's *The Crying of Lot 49,* and Kurt Vonnegut's *Cat's Cradle.*

My desire throughout the four subsequent chapters devoted to critical analyses is to allow the works to speak for themselves. Concentrating in each case on a close reading of the text, I hope that the integral structure of the novel's symbolism will thereby be disclosed. No attempt will be made to complete the typology of apocalypse until the task of describing the symbolic structures of the novels has been finished. Only in chapter 6, therefore, will an assessment be made of the indebtedness, varieties, and innovations of the American tradition of literary apocalypse.

CHAPTER TWO

The Possibility of Renewal:

The Ideal and the Real in Hawthorne, Melville, and Twain

The Blithedale Romance (1852), *The Confidence-Man* (1857), and *The Mysterious Stranger* (1916), when considered together, afford instructive insights into the eschatological sensibilities of their respective authors and into their attitudes toward change and history reflected in the imagery and structure of the novels. *The Blithedale Romance* and *The Confidence-Man* have settings contemporary with their composition; *The Mysterious Stranger*, although set in sixteenth-century Austria, ranges freely through time and space. Hawthorne draws material from his stay at Brook Farm in 1841. The "Blithedale" of the romance is "a faint and not very faithful shadowing of Brook Farm,"[1] he avers in the preface. Melville's *The Confidence-Man* is a dawn-to-midnight April Fools' Day journey down the Mississippi River aboard the steamer *Fidèle* with a cross section of mid-century Americans, published coincidentally on April 1, 1857. To soften the harsh philosophy of his old age

Twain deceptively employs a characteristic nostalgia for youth and a curious medieval setting: an Austrian town—appropriately called Eseldorf (Assville)—in the remote past of our belief.

Each of the works presently under consideration, although employing symbols and structures that are specifically apocalyptic, is particularly pertinent because, in vastly different ways, they are concerned with the very problem raised and resolved by Judaeo-Christian apocalypse. The Book of Revelation instructs the believer to expect the agony of continued conflict rather than the beatitude of easy victory. Each of these works reacts against the facile optimism of nineteenth-century America. Manifest destiny was after all a secularized statement of Christian millenarianism. Hawthorne, Melville, and Twain raise the question of the meaning of history and the possibility of genuine renewal of human life. How does the ideal relate to human existence? Does one reform history by separating oneself from its mainstream? Or does one realize the ideal of human existence simply through the acceptance of the way of Christian charity? Perhaps one can avoid misery and achieve requisite happiness through the preservation of the innocent exuberance of childhood.

Each author in his own way resolves the tension between the ideal and the real, between the pursuit of reform and the tyranny of history, between the desire for happiness and human existence as it is experienced. Hawthorne, while seeming to affirm the quest for the ideal, questions the possibility of seeking it apart from the real order of human events. Melville explores his characteristic skepticism, the impossibility of realizing the ideal as embodied in Christianity, granted the appalling weakness of human nature. Twain laughs at both the ideal and the real.

I

A landmark in the criticism of *The Blithedale Romance* was undoubtedly Frederick Crews's 1957 essay which shows that it is not so much the "story" but rather the act of telling it that is important.[2] Other critiques have dwelled upon the artist's dilemma as a central theme of the romance, reflected in narrator Coverdale's consciousness of his curiosity as well as his distance as observer. As Peter Murray has commented, Coverdale "holds himself aloof so that he may the better act as an interpreter of the action,"[3] yet to be creative he must also "live in other lives . . . to learn the secret which was hidden even from themselves" (p. 173). Criticism, moreover, has clearly established the distinction that must be made between the raw material of the romance—Blithedale as an experiment in reform and community—and the meaning of the romance discovered in and through Miles Coverdale. In investigating Hawthorne's attitude toward the possibility of realizing the ideal, I will focus attention primarily on the imagery of the novel, within the framework of the levels of meaning extracted by the criticism to date, but in this order: the artistic dilemma of the narrator, the interaction of the principal characters of the Blithedale experiment, and the significance of the very act itself of telling the romance.

Coverdale refers to his subordination to the principal actors in the Blithedale drama as resembling "that of the Chorus in a classic play" (p. 116). This is the way Coverdale thinks of himself in relation to Hollingsworth, Zenobia, and Priscilla—and to a lesser extent to Westervelt and Moodie. He defines his posture as chorus in terms of being aloof from personal involvement, yet with an emotional state proportioned to the fortunes of the others. The artist's dilemma is that he must stand apart, yet be a keen observer. (Coverdale acknowledges toward the end of his tale that he has been ranked high, by one critic at least, among the minor poets of the period.)

The four window scenes in the romance become symbolic of artistic distance. In the first, Moodie desires to see Zenobia holding Priscilla's hand, seeking some assurance that there is an affection growing between them. Hollingsworth directs Moodie to a vantage point, and later Coverdale observes Moodie "behind the trunk of a tree, gazing earnestly towards a particular window of the farm-house; and, by and by, Priscilla appeared at this window, playfully drawing along Zenobia" (p. 108). Old Moodie is distressed, though, when Zenobia puts Priscilla off, perhaps because the latter has taken too great a liberty. The second window scene concerns Coverdale himself spying on Priscilla from his hermitage in the woods. Although he is some distance away, he is assured that it is Priscilla "sitting at Zenobia's window, and making little purses" (p. 119). The third reference to windows occurs when Coverdale observes the boardinghouse to the rear of his hotel. In the drawing-room window, he sees Zenobia joined by Westervelt; a narrower window to the left shows Priscilla "in airy drapery" (p. 168), engaged in her handiwork. Zenobia later signs her recognition of the spying Coverdale by dropping the curtain. In the fourth and final use of the window, Coverdale throws a tuft of grass through Hollingsworth's window and scarcely a moment passes before the latter looks out. Coverdale has come to alert him concerning the suspicions of Zenobia's suicide.

The references to windows support the motif of Coverdale's experience of artistic distance; the same is true of the explicit stage scene when Hollingsworth rescues Priscilla from Westervelt and Coverdale is simply a part of the audience. Nevertheless, Coverdale's gradual assumption of a role of prominence in the window scenes parallels symbolically his increasing involvement in the Blithedale drama; indeed, his increased knowledge of the participants makes him more a part of their tragedy. In the first window scene it is Moodie who is the principal viewer, and Coverdale observes the framed sisters indirectly through him. In the second scene Coverdale alone and from a distance observes what he feels sure is Priscilla. He remarks, "Though a great way off, the eye of faith assured me that it was she" (p. 119). In the third scene Coverdale not only sees others, but is observed by them as well. And in the final scene Coverdale communicates through what was formerly a symbol of distance when he demands Hollingsworth's attention to Zenobia's plight.

This strand of imagery, it seems to me, relates primarily to Coverdale's personal dilemma as artist. Insofar as

it addresses itself to the tension between involvement
and distance, the imagery is a particular reflection of the
more generalized problem of reform. True art, as Coverdale eventually acknowledges, is a blend of the ideal
and the real; the indication of progressive involvement
in the window images shows his gradual realization that
artistic creation is sterile apart from the real. As we continue analyzing the levels of meaning in the novel,
though, it is nevertheless clear that the images concerned
with Coverdale's dilemma must be distinguished carefully from those related to the actual interaction of the
personages in the adventure which is Blithedale itself.
Aware of the allowances that we must make for Coverdale's fanciful curiosity and even cynical humor at
times, we can approach the meaning of Blithedale. The
tone of Coverdale's remembrance is at best playful when
he recalls that he had left his "cosey pair of bachelor-
rooms . . . and plunged into the heart of the pitiless
snowstorm, in quest of a better life" (p. 38). Blithedale
is intended to be "for the reformation of the world"
(p. 40) and not just for the benefit of the participants.

The chapter significantly entitled "A Knot of Dream-
ers" gives perhaps the most elaborate description of the
venture. The group had left "the rusty iron frame-work
of society, . . . the weary tread-mill of the established
system" (p. 46). Coverdale defines their ambition: "It
was our purpose—a generous one, certainly, and absurd,
no doubt, in full proportion with its generosity—to give
up whatever we had heretofore attained, for the sake
of showing mankind the example of a life governed by
other than the false and cruel principles on which

human society has all along been based" (p. 46). Replacing pride with "familiar love," the Blithedalers sought "to offer up the earnest toil of [their] bodies, as a prayer no less than an effort for the advancement of our race" (p. 47). The emphasis on "familiar love" is reminiscent of John Winthrop's famous sermon aboard the flagship *Arbella*, although the love that Coverdale describes would seem now to be stripped of any religious significance. Coverdale, no doubt ironically, uses an image that was a favorite analogy of the early Puritans. He expresses the hope that their "blazing windows will be visible a great way off" (p. 51). John Winthrop had proclaimed with deadly seriousness: "For we must consider that we shall be as a city upon a hill, the eyes of all people are upon us."[4] That the Puritans considered themselves to be a model for the future reformation of the world is clear from Winthrop's imagined prayer of succeeding plantations: "The Lord make it like that of New England."[5]

The Blithedalers were pilgrims striving "towards the millennium of love" (p. 51), but like most utopians they had so confounded humility with a sense of election that they were able to claim that their "present bivouac was considerably further into the waste of chaos than any mortal army of crusaders had ever marched before" (p. 76)—or at least this is the way Coverdale mixes cynicism with fact. Their enterprise for the reformation of the world was inextricably bound up, in theory at least, "with delectable visions of the spiritualization of labor" (p. 87). But in a moment of reminiscence that probably comes closer to the truth about Coverdale and the other visionaries than any of his other reflections, he admits that the group's bond was negative rather than affirmative: "We had individually found one thing or another to quarrel with in our past life, and were pretty well agreed as to the inexpediency of lumbering along with the old system any further" (p. 85). They had as a matter of fact each joined the group for ulterior motives.

The typology that Hawthorne employs through Coverdale for describing Blithedale's intended reformation of society is taken from the Genesis account of origins. When Coverdale recalls the warmth of the hearth on the day of his arrival, it is with the realization that the snowstorm has "exploded [their] scheme for beginning the life of Paradise anew" (p. 37). The explicit references to Eden, therefore, are usually by way of contrast with the reality of their situation. Coverdale notes with pity that they are unable to exclude housework from their system, even though the absence of housework distinguished Eden from later, artificial societies. "Eve," Coverdale reminds Zenobia, "had no dinner-pot, and no clothes to mend, and no washing-day." Zenobia answers "with mirth gleaming out of her eyes, 'We shall find some difficulty in adopting the Paradisiacal system for at least a month to come. . . . As for the garb of Eden, . . . I shall not assume it till after May-Day'" (p. 44). And in a curious lapse of his customary reserve that could conceivably be humorously construed as Hawthorne's early connivance with the demon of American pornography, Coverdale imagines Zenobia's "fine, perfectly developed figure, in Eve's earliest garment" (p.

44). He modestly attributes the image to the defect of his own imagination rather than to Zenobia's intentions. A little later though, despite his protestations, Coverdale seems almost like a "backslider" when he imagines a marble sculpture of Zenobia "with the utmost scantiness of drapery, so that the eye might chastely be gladdened with her material perfection in its entireness" (p. 68).

Coverdale's recollection of his initial impression of the power of Zenobia's personality is described in terms of Eve: "One felt an influence breathing out of her such as we might suppose to come from Eve, when she was just made, and her Creator brought her to Adam, saying, 'Behold! here is a woman!'" (p. 45). After Coverdale's illness and return to health, his enthusiasm transforms the earth and its inhabitants, but the transformation sounds more like the old creation: "Man looked strong and stately,—and woman, O how beautiful!—and the earth a green garden, blossoming with many-colored delights" (p. 84). Later in Coverdale's narrative there is irony in his realization of the curse of Adam in a place that was intended to be Eden itself: "The curse of Adam's posterity—and, curse or blessing be it, it gives substance to the life around us—had first come upon me there. In the sweat of my brow I had there earned bread and eaten it, and so established my claim to be on earth, and my fellowship with all the sons of labor" (pp. 213–14).

References to Westervelt as the tempter of the Eden legend are less explicit, but nontheless certain. His first appearance, which is unexpected enough for Coverdale to consider it an apparition, occurs in "dim woodland solitude" (p. 111). In addition to the fact that he is "as handsome a man" as Coverdale has ever seen, his hair, beard, and mustache are "coal-black," and his eyes too are "black and sparkling." The wooden head of his walking stick is "carved in vivid imitation of that of a serpent" (p. 112). While he conversed with Coverdale, "his black eyes sparkled . . . as if the devil were peeping out of them" (p. 114). His laugh is brief and metallic. Coverdale sees Westervelt's smile that reveals his false teeth as the mark of his demonic connections: "Every human being, when given over to the devil, is sure to have the wizard mark upon him, in one form or another. I fancied that this smile, with its peculiar revelation, was the devil's signet on the Professor" (p. 171). Later when Westervelt enters the drawing room, Coverdale senses his dislike for him as "a creeping of the flesh, as when, feeling about in a dark place, one touches something cold and slimy, and questions what the secret hatefulness may be" (p. 184). Westervelt is of course a mesmerist and much of the description is appropriate to that kind of life of mystery, but underlying the evil visage of the enchanter are definite suggestions of a more primitive, demonic type.

But the return to origins, done significantly although often just facetiously in imagery from the garden of Eden, is nothing more than a masquerade; the sought-after reformation is ineffectual because it is only a surface thing. And here I refer specifically to the repeated references to masks, which I consider to be not a support to the imagery of artistic distance as in chorus, window, and stage, but rather a direct statement about the

illusory nature of the personal drama that erupts at
Blithedale. Daniel Hoffman has suggested that "Blithedale . . . believes in the great American comic possibility,
rebirth without death."[6] And it is this comic possibility
that he sees symbolized by the repeated mask imagery:
"We may now see that the main theme of abortive
rebirth is dramatized through the pervasive rituals of
masquerade and metamorphosis. . . . *All* of the characters are in one way or another wearing masks. . . .
Their perpetual masquerade hides their true identities
fom one another."[7] Hoffman's analysis, however perceptive, is concerned with Blithedale. Yet the references to
the masquerade, although centered upon the interaction
at Blithedale, go beyond the actual group of intended
reformers. Literally *all* of the principal characters in the
romance are somehow represented as concealing themselves, and not just from Coverdale. Their true purposes
are indeed hidden from each other. We are dealing here
therefore with an entirely different facet of the work
from the question of the artist's dilemma. In the light
of the fact that the masquerade extends beyond Blithedale, it would seem that Hoffman's analysis must be
extended as well. To conceal oneself is to deny reality.
Thus the masquerade in Hawthorne's romance is a metaphor for those who seek change apart from reality, from
history. And Blithedale itself, understood now as more
than just reform of society, becomes a metaphor for the
illusory quest of an ideal outside of the mainstream
of history.

The Veiled Lady, mentioned in the very first sentence
of the novel, becomes a mysterious yet all-encompassing

reminder of the more subtle masquerade that each of the characters is engaged in. Just as her veil literally covers her "from head to foot" (p. 34), so the principal characters of the romance have purposely hidden their ulterior motives behind the veil of reform. Zenobia's name, which is "merely her public name," is "a sort of mask in which she comes before the world, retaining all the privileges of privacy,—a contrivance, in short, like the white drapery of the Veiled Lady, only a little more transparent" (p. 36). Less transparent than the name is the tropical flower that she wears in her hair and changes daily. Zenobia calls it a relic of her earlier, happier days: Coverdale suggests to Hollingsworth that she "is an enchantress" and that the "flower in her hair is a talisman" (p. 69). The first evening at Blithedale, when Zenobia discards her languid flower, Coverdale, who certainly should never have been the first to cast a stone, is provoked to judge her: "The presence of Zenobia caused our heroic enterprise to show like an illusion, a masquerade, a pastoral, a counterfeit Arcadia, in which we grown-up men and women were making a playday of the years that were given us to live in" (p. 48). The purses with concealed openings that Priscilla knits are "a symbol of Priscilla's own mystery" (p. 60). The dark frown that disfigures Hollingsworth's brow is an occasional suggestion of the dark side of his intentions. Zenobia finally pronounces judgment on Hollingsworth's duplicity: "Self, self, self! You have embodied yourself in a project. You are a better masquerader than the witches and gypsies yonder; for your disguise is a self-deception" (p. 224). Coverdale's hermitage in the woods is his "one

exclusive possession" (p. 118); it helps him to keep
inviolate the individuality that it symbolizes. Actually,
it is an elaborate concealment of his spying and a symbol
of his own insatiable curiosity as artist in search of
fresh material.

Westervelt is not part of the experimental reform of
Blithedale, but he is a crucial though totally mysterious
part of the drama of personal domination that masquer-
ades as reformation of society and of which Blithedale
becomes the symbol. Coverdale conjectures that the
wonderful beauty of his face may, after all, "be remov-
able like a mask" (p. 115). The gold band supporting
his false teeth is symbolic of the evil that lurks behind
the glittering facade of his smile. And Moodie, who is
so anxious to conceal his purpose throughout the greater
part of the story, wears a patch over one eye. Moodie
likewise is apart from the actual experiment, but clearly
part of the comic attempt at rebirth without suffering.
"He had," Coverdale notes, "a queer appearance of hid-
ing himself behind the patch on his left eye" (p. 103).

That Blithedale itself refers not so much to reform
as to the interaction of the principal characters, using
each other for their own ulterior purposes, and that the
veil is its symbol, is supported by the fact that Silas Foster,
who is the backbone of the experiment in utopian community, is never referred to as disguised in any way.
"Grim Silas Foster," as Coverdale calls him, is the steady,
stolid, plodding Yankee worker who takes up at Blithedale where he left off before agreeing to manage the
farm and instruct the group. He is reality come to
Blithedale. Silas always cuts through the dream world

of facile reform and factitious beatitude with his simple reminders about the way things are. When Coverdale imagines the fire of their first night's hearth as a beacon kindled for humanity, Silas observes that the "blaze of that brush-wood will only last a minute or two longer" (pp. 51–52). And in the fall when Coverdale returns to Blithedale and encounters the group masquerading in the woods, "as if Comus and his crew were holding their revels," it is Silas who disrupts the unity of the pageant: "But Silas Foster, who leaned against a tree near by, in his customary blue frock, and smoking a short pipe, did more to disenchant the scene, with his look of shrewd, acrid, Yankee observation, than twenty witches and necromancers could have done in the way of rendering it weird and fantastic" (pp. 216–17).

But the prevailing symbol of the romance is the veil. As Frank Davidson has pointed out, it is every bit as real and complex as Hawthorne's scarlet A.[8] It reminds us constantly of the illusory nature of the quest for the ideal apart from the real; such an effort is never more than a mask concealing our real selves, and it is doomed to failure.

It is certainly not seeking the ideal that Hawthorne sees as catastrophic; rather seeking it apart from the real is what is open to condemnation. In the American experience, the quest for the ideal apart from the mainstream of life was not true of all Puritans by any means, but it was apparently of "the purest of the purifiers,"[9] as Perry Miller has called the separatist settlers of Plymouth plantation. Miller suggests, too, that because they had withdrawn they were "able to concentrate upon the essence of Puritanism."[10] William Bradford's history of Plymouth begins with the call that the original group received before leaving England, and already the tone of separatist reform is established: "When as by the travail and diligence of some godly and zealous preachers, and God's blessing on their labors, . . . many became enlightened by the word of God and had their ignorance and sins discovered unto them, and began by His grace to reform their lives and make conscience of their ways: the work of God was no sooner manifest in them but presently they were both scoffed and scorned by the profane multitude."[11]

In *The Blithedale Romance* Hollingsworth is drawn most explicitly in Puritan images. Originally a blacksmith, he looks older than his thirty years, "with his great shaggy head, his heavy brow, his dark complexion, his abundant beard, and the rude strength with which his features seemed to have been hammered out of iron" (p. 54). Hollingsworth himself uses the image of iron: "I have always been in earnest. . . . I have hammered thought out of iron, after heating the iron in my heart" (p. 90). Iron is of course a characteristic Hawthornian image for the Puritan. In "The Maypole of Merry Mount," not only are the Puritans' weapons ("always at hand") made of iron, but their leader John Endicott seems "wrought of iron" too, so stern is every aspect of the man—"visage, frame, and soul."[12]

Hollingsworth admits that the marked characteristic of his personality "is an inflexible severity of purpose" (p. 67). His philanthropic desire is to build an edifice dedicated to "the reform and mental culture" (p. 79) of criminals; indeed his sole purpose for coming to Blithedale is apparently to proselytize for his cause. Hollingsworth wants his building to be "a spectacle to the world, . . . that it may take example and build many another like it" (p. 101–2) ; and so he intends to "set it on the open hill-side," a purpose clearly reminiscent of the heavenly city that the Puritans were bringing to the shore of New England. Coverdale feels in retrospect that Hollingsworth's "prolonged fiddling upon one string" (p. 79) was the main reason for his incipient insanity at the time. Zenobia calls him "a cold, heartless, self-beginning and self-ending piece of mechanism" (p. 224), and Coverdale confides that he is "not altogether human" (p. 92).

Two significant scenes of the romance are set at Eliot's pulpit, a rock near the farmhouse that tradition claimed the apostle Eliot had used in preaching to the Indians. The inner group is accustomed to meet there on Sundays, and Hollingsworth is in the habit of mounting the rock to lecture to his friends. The connection with tradition is made explicit by Coverdale: "Our Sundays, at Blithedale, were not ordinarily kept with such rigid observance as might have befitted the descendants of the Pilgrims, whose high enterprise, as we sometimes flattered ourselves, we had taken up, and were carrying it onward and aloft, to a point which they never dreamed of attaining" (p. 134). Both scenes, perhaps because of the aura of sacredness associated with the place, are occasions of judgment and revelation. In the first, Hollingsworth reveals his unalterable opposition to Zenobia's view of woman; the second is concerned with the effects of Hollingsworth's final judgment of Zenobia as unfit to be his companion. Coverdale sees Hollingsworth on that occasion as "all that an artist could desire for the grim portrait of a Puritan magistrate holding inquest of life and death in a case of witchcraft" (pp. 220–21).

Coverdale's final description of the broken Hollingsworth, spending his life with Priscilla in the reform of just one criminal, himself—for he blames himself for Zenobia's suicide—is so similar in tone to the resolution of the conflict of "The Maypole of Merry Mount" that it can hardly be coincidental. It's rather a fortunate recurrence of the realistic vision that we associate with Hawthorne's literary and religious genius. The irony of *The Blithedale Romance*, as Daniel Hoffman has pointed out, is that Hawthorne has placed the representative of duty and gloom, Hollingsworth, *within* the new Merry Mount. At the end of the romance, the once proud Hollingsworth manifests "a self-distrustful weakness, and a childlike or childish tendency to press close, and closer still, to the side of the slender woman whose arm was within his" (p. 246).

It is the Lord and Lady of the May who capture our attention at the conclusion of "The Maypole of Merry Mount." Even before Endicott blesses their marriage by throwing the wreath of roses over their heads, it is clear that the real hope of the New World lies with them because they alone suspect and seem to be resigned to the ambiguity that is the inevitable result of human interaction. For we are told that "from the moment that they *truly loved*, they had subjected themselves to earth's doom of care and sorrow, and *troubled joy*, and had no

more a home at Merry Mount."[13] Confronted by Endicott, they hold each other "with weight enough to
express that their destinies were linked together, for good
or evil."[14] When Endicott himself finally joins them
together with the wreath, Hawthorne calls it a "deed of
prophecy,"[15] suggesting that the ultimate resolution of
the conflict between moral gloom and systematic gaiety
will be worked out through human interdependence in
an atmosphere of "troubled joy." This final phrase situates Hawthorne's response to the tensions in his story in
the gray area of life that is east of Eden, where neither
uninhibited joy nor depressing gloom reigns.

Hoffman claims that Hollingsworth's is "the typically
Puritan sin of intellectual pride, mistaking his own sel-
fish purpose for the moral imperative of the universe."[16]
Pride seems somewhat harsh; to confuse one's program
of reform with the will of God is certainly an excess of
religious zeal, perhaps even simple intolerance. And the
Puritans through their covenant theology did confuse
their plans with God's design. John Winthrop, in that
sermon mentioned earlier, praises God for the covenant
He has made with them, but adds for clarification: "The
Lord hath given us leave to draw our own articles."[17]
Hoffman is more accurate, therefore, about Hollingsworth than he is concerning Puritan fault.

On a more fundamental level, however, Hollingsworth and the separatist Puritans had the same problem:
divorcing the ideal from the real. And it is this that
Hawthorne sees as doomed to disaster. Although Hollingsworth, alone among the principals of Blithedale, is
explicitly drawn in Puritan images, the separation of

the ideal from the real is equally applicable as fault to Coverdale's writing of the romance and to Zenobia's drive toward the new feminine ideal. In striving to present humanity "with an indescribable ideal charm," the justification of his romance, Coverdale failed to give us "the genuine article" (p. 186). The virtues of the personages are the figments of a detached fancy and never qualities of real people. And, to press her ideal, Zenobia had to entertain an image of herself as thoroughly independent; yet so needy is she, suicide is the only option when Hollingsworth is no longer available. None of them of course is actually a Puritan, but they have all inherited the original sin of the land—they tried to divorce change from history.

Within the threefold framework of the constitutive symbolism of apocalypse, catastrophe in *The Blithedale Romance* is drawn in the microcosmic terms of the dissolution of the Blithedale experiment. Zenobia's suicide typifies the defeat that lies in wait for reformers who separate themselves from society. The masks that are worn by the characters in their charade of mutual deception are symbolic of the chaos of the evil age preceding the end. The veil is actually a symbol both of warning and of judgment. The reform of Blithedale is a mere masquerade because each of the participants seeks change despite the unreformed self that lurks behind the mask of facile optimism. The imagery of paradise is also part of the symbolism of judgment; its use is ironical because the paradisiacal images always stand in marked contrast to the reality of life at Blithedale.

The portrait of Hollingsworth as a Puritan reveals the

unreformed center of his heart. It reflects also a judgment of separatist Puritanism which divorced reform from the mainsteam of history. The reformer is an artist of sorts; he must stand far enough away from what is to be reformed to be able to see the total picture. Yet distance, as in the window imagery of the romance, can mean simple separation or even alienation from the very thing that is to be reformed. Thus the window imagery insofar as it means separation is related to the symbolism of judgment.

Hollingsworth and Priscilla, who come together finally to reform one man's heart, represent the modest possibility of genuine renewal that Hawthorne envisions in his romance. Reform begins with oneself; it proceeds from that source almost imperceptibly.

II

In analyzing *The Confidence-Man*, I will be concerned with structure as well as imagery. The novel's structure and imagery, I hope to demonstrate, are both significantly apocalyptic. In fact, the tone set by the apocalyptic images of the novel is crucial for analyzing the structure underlying the appearances of the confidence man. The conclusion that only detailed textual analysis will support is that there are seven disguises of the confidence man, following the appearance of Christ as the deaf-mute.[18] Seven is of course an apocalyptic symbol of completion. The appearances of the confidence man, moreover, represent the last loosing of Satan, the classic Christian sign of the imminent end of the world. In

showing mankind either immune to or a victim of the
wiles of his loosed Satan, Melville doubts the very possibility of the ideal of charity among men.

No commentator actually presents sufficient detail
related to the number of guises to make his conclusion
acceptable. R. W. B. Lewis, for example, one of those
claiming that "the Confidence Man makes eight appearances in all," simply notes that "Melville helps us detect
the so-to-speak genuine masks of the Confidence Man
by a number of devices: for example, by showing the
man with the weed in possession of a business card we
have seen Black Guinea surreptitiously acquiring; by
having the various personae loudly vouch for each other;
by a similarity of names—John Ringman (a man who is
a ringer of changes), John Truman, Frank Goodman."[19]
The only key that works through at least seven guises,
however, is the second that Lewis offers, the personae
vouching for each other. Yet no combination of clues
will yield the conclusion that he draws. There is simply
no way of connecting the deaf-mute with the subsequent confidence men, except that they all refer to
charity in one form or another; but that is hardly a connecting link because everyone in the novel talks about
charity. The deaf-mute obviously does not vouch for
anyone because he is mute; and not a single one of the
personae, from Black Guinea through the cosmopolitan,
gives any indication that he "knows" the deaf-mute in
the way the seven refer to each other.

That the man in cream-colors, the deaf-mute, represents the advent of Christ seems clear from the text. He
"appears" at "sunrise" and is described as coming "sud-

denly as Manco Capac at the lake Titicaca."[20] The sud-
denness of the deaf-mute's arrival, therefore, suggests a
theophany. In the allegorical time of the novel, his
appearance at sunrise contrasts perfectly with the total
darkness of the end—a midnight world surrendered to
evil. White and gold are the colors associated with the
deaf-mute. "His cheek was fair, his chin downy, his hair
flaxen, his hat a white fur one, with a long fleecy nap."
He is unencumbered by baggage or friends. He is greeted
by "shrugged shoulders, titters, whispers, wonderings of
the crowd," and the author notes that it is clear that he
is "in the extremest sense of the word, a stranger" (p. 9).
A further comment is made that the deaf-mute "seemed
already to have come from a very long distance" (p.
12). Already there are intimations of Melville's characteristic concern with the inoperability of Christianity.
As Plotinus Plinlimmon's pamphlet in *Pierre* puts it,
God's laws make as much sense on earth as Greenwich
mean time would in China.

After writing verses from Paul's hymn to charity on
a slate, a message that meets with stares, jeers, pushes, and
punches, he retires to the forecastle and goes to sleep,
"his whole lamb-like figure relaxed" (p. 12). We are
treated then to a list of "epitaphic comments" from the
crowd, the last of which compares him significantly to
"Jacob dreaming at Luz" (p. 13). The deaf-mute has
gone to sleep at "the foot of a ladder . . . leading to a
deck above" (p. 12), and it was of course at Luz that
Jacob dreamt that he saw a ladder going from earth to
heaven (Gen. 28:10–19). Jacob, one of the patriarchs,
is also clearly a type of Christ; the irony of Melville's

reference undoubtedly lies in the fact that God speaking
to Jacob at Luz promised the land to his descendants,
who were to be "countless as the dust upon the earth"
(Gen. 28:14). So after the brief passage of the deaf-
mute among the crowds on the *Fidèle*—a "flock of fools,
under this captain of fools, in this ship of fools!" (p.
21)—false prophets of mindless confidence are his only
apparent descendants. We can only conjecture that
Melville wanted his Christ figure a deaf-mute to set him
apart from the crowd, to contrast him with the confidence men who are anything but mute, and perhaps also
to suggest paradoxically that Christ could not have heard
the response to his impracticable doctrine.

It is typical of Melville and of his preoccupation with
the ambiguity of life that a considerable vagueness should
exist in the description of the maneuvers of the confidence man. When Black Guinea insists that there are
"ever so many good, kind, honest ge'mmen" (p. 19)
who would vouch for him, and then mentions eight, we
may expect, if Melville were not the author, to meet
them all in successive episodes. Only five however appear
in the direct line of those mutually vouching for each
other: the man with the weed, John Ringman; the gentleman with the gray coat and white tie, agent of the
Widow and Orphan Asylum for Seminoles; John Truman, the gentleman with the traveling-cap and ledger,
president and transfer agent of the Black Rapids Coal
Company; the herb-doctor, in the snuff-colored surtout;
and the gentleman with the brass-plate, from the Philosophical Intelligence Office. The three others that Black
Guinea mentions—"a ge'mman in a yaller west; . . . and

a ge'mman in a wiolet robe; and a ge'mman as is a sodjer'
(p. 19)—appear at first to have no counterparts in the
unfolding of the April Fools' Day trip aboard the *Fidèle*.
Yet the juvenile peddler of the last chapter, selling
traveler's locks, moneybelts, and Counterfeit Detectors,
is dressed "in the fragment of an old linen coat, bedrag-
gled and yellow" (p. 252). Charles Arnold Noble, who
explains the metaphysics of indian-hating and later
retires at the suggestion of the cosmopolitan, is wearing
"a violet vest" (p. 147). And Thomas Fry, whom the
herb-doctor calls a soldier of fortune (p. 105), admits
that most people do not believe his story of the injustice
he has been the victim of and says, "So to most I tell a
different one" (p. 104). Even though these latter three
"ge'mmen" interact with the major masks of the confidence man, they are made from the same mold and could
readily vouch for Black Guinea because they live the
same lie. Clearly they are already accomplished confidence men themselves; and so they are worthy, in the
words of James Miller, to appear "in the list of the
devil's minions."[21]

Black Guinea mentions five of the principal personae;
he omits only the cosmopolitan, who is after all the rain-
bow blend of all the disguises. John Ringman, the man
with the weed, tells Henry Roberts, the country merchant, that he knows the poor crippled Negro well (p.
25) and announces that the president of the Black
Rapids Coal Company has some stock to dispose of (p.
29). The man in gray coat and white tie claims to have
assisted Black Guinea ashore, when the clergyman
inquires about him (p. 36). The man in traveling-cap

and ledger, president and transfer agent of the Coal
Company, tells the sophomore he has seen the man with
the weed (p. 53), but to the country merchant denies
knowing either Ringman or the cripple (p. 65). He
does, however, tell the miser that the herb-doctor is his
friend (p. 80). The herb-doctor seeks out the agent of
the Seminole Widow and Orphan Asylum to make a
contribution (p. 96), tells crippled Thomas Fry that his
legs are similar to Black Guinea's (p. 106), and alone
refers to the president of the Coal Company by the
name John Truman (p. 109). The man with the brass-
plate thinks that, as he was boarding at Cape Giradeau,
he saw the herb-doctor going ashore (p. 121). And,
finally, the cosmopolitan, having overheard the Intelligence Office man, or so he claims, considers him "a rather
sensible fellow" (p. 141).

The conclusive reason why there should be seven peddlers of practical confidence, no more and no less, derives
from the emphasis on apocalypse in the final chapter.
Although humor pervades the novel—Melville himself
labels it "a work of amusement" (p. 190)—there is a
strong base of ironic seriousness supporting the tale; it is
so strong that Daniel Hoffman can call *The Confidence-
Man* "a despairing book, a bitter book, a work of Byzan-
tine ingenuity" and a "merciless apocalypse."[22] Merciless
or not, it is apocalypse in tone as well as in structure.
Biblical student that he was, Melville had to be aware in
the light of his concluding references to apocalypse that
he had been framing his fantasy of the last loosing of
Satan within the primary numerical symbolism of the
Book of Revelation. The number seven is symbolic of

completion. Thus when the cosmopolitan—the seventh and longest disguise of the confidence man—exits into darkness, we should know that there is no more, that we have witnessed at least in fantasy the end of the American world of the *Fidèle*.

The indications are clear that the references in the final chapter are to the New Testament apocalypse. On the shade of the solar lamp in the gentlemen's cabin, "the image of a horned altar, from which flames rose, alternate[s] with the figure of a robed man, his head encircled by a halo" (p. 247). Considered alone, the reference to the robed man with the halo could be almost any Christian saint (Rev. 6:9–11), but together with the horned altar (Rev. 8:3, 9:13) it almost certainly refers to the popular but traditional association of the John of Revelation with St. John the apostle and evangelist. The other lamps in the cabin are "barren planets, which had either gone out from exhaustion, or been extinguished" (pp. 247–48). The partial extinction of sun, moon, and stars is an image of apocalypse associated with the angel of the fourth trumpet (Rev. 8:12). Complete darkness, symbolic of chaos, is the ultimate announcement of the end. Thus gradually the solar lamp "begins to burn dimly" (p. 259) until the cosmopolitan finally extinguishes it altogether and leads the old man away in darkness.

The old man seated at the table "keeping his lone vigils beneath his lone lamp" has "a countenance like that which imagination ascribes to good Simeon, when, having at last beheld the Master of Faith, he blessed him and departed in peace" (p. 248). Only Melville could have perpetrated the irony of an aged Simeon waiting to bless

his savior and instead being led off into the darkness by
Satan himself—in sheep's clothing, of course.

The sound of voices—voices of revelation and warning—is a recurring image in the Book of Revelation. In
the final chapter of *The Confidence-Man*, a voice comes
from a berth four times, and what it says sounds more like
the essence of Melville than the idle prattle of a sleeper,
as the confidence man would have the old man believe.
When the old man objects to the eager stare of the confidence man, as if it were wartime and he had the only
copy of a newspaper with good news (when actually he
is reading the Bible), the cosmopolitan says, "And so
you *have* good news there, sir—the very best of good
news." The voice from one of the curtained berths comments, "Too good to be true" (p. 249). Melville, who
began the novel by calling the deaf-mute Christ a
stranger "in the extremest sense of the word," ends with
a succinct reminder of the impracticality of Christianity. The teaching of Jesus is simply too good to be practiced, at least by man as we know him. This is borne out
in *The Confidence-Man* as we see America aboard the
Fidèle duped constantly into a facile optimism that is
mistaken for the genuine message of Jesus.

When the cosmopolitan says that he was surprised to
find it written in the Bible, as he had been warned, that
"an enemy speaketh sweetly with his lips," the voice
asks, "Who's that describing the confidence-man?" (pp.
249–50). In his many guises he had indeed spoken
sweetly, but his words were all false, as Daniel Hoffman
has observed so pointedly: "The con man . . . confuses
every moral issue he touches, dissuading well-meaning

persons from the instinctual truth of their hearts' wisdom; he quotes Scripture to lead them into darkness."[23] The old man reminds the cosmospolitan that the verses he refers to are from Sirach, an apocryphal book and therefore "something of uncertain credit" (p. 250). Hearing the word "apocrypha," the voice from the berth asks, "What's that about the Apocalypse?" (p. 251). The implication is clear; if man persists in facile confidence, he is indeed inviting catastrophe. Then the cosmopolitan chatters on about never reading "anything so calculated to destroy man's confidence in man" (p. 251) as that passage from the Wisdom of Jesus Son of Sirach; the voice interrupts a fourth and final time, in jest now rather than mockery, to suggest that they go find wisdom between their blankets and not keep wiser men awake.

Although the confidence man in his various guises has extraordinary success in duping passengers into accepting his doctrine of unquestioning confidence in their fellow men, particularly in him, there are four who resist his sweet logic: the wooden-legged man, who is bent on proving Black Guinea to be "some white operator, betwisted and painted up for a decoy" (p. 20); the dusk giant, who calls the herb-doctor a "profane fiddler on heart-strings" (p. 94); and finally Mark Winsome and Egbert, who really ought to be counted as one, since they stand to each other as theory to practice. Melville, refusing as always to make it easy to arrange his world into a neat structure, refrains from having his loosed Satan totally successful. Yet a closer analysis shows that these four are revealed by the confidence man to be beyond temptation because they have already lost their humanity. Pitch, the Missouri bachelor, who professes "confidence in distrust" (p. 115) and almost remains consistent with his view of total human depravity, yields finally to the man with the brass-plate, apparently because his vanity has been touched (p. 137).

The four who resist completely are all "brother stranger[s]" (p. 203) to the confidence man; they are his opposites and as such have already sinned in the other extreme. Daniel Hoffman observes: "Their faith in heartless self-reliance complements his in indiscriminate confidence. His makes no room in the moral universe for evil, theirs leaves none for good."[24] Although Hoffman is speaking simply of Mark Winsome—almost consistently taken by the critics to be Melville's caricature of Emerson—and his disciple Egbert, his judgment applies as well to the wooden-legged man and the dusk giant, who simply represent the same philosophy reduced to uncouth practice.

Although references to Satan and related images would hardly be proof that Melville wanted his confidence man to be taken for the devil, there are enough to suggest that any interpretation short of the demonic would distort the text. There can be no doubt that the message of the confidence man is a sheer perversion of Christianity. Black Guinea, the "grotesque negro cripple" (p. 16), who names all those who will vouch for him, knows the extent of his demonic power as well as the limits of his satanic legion. John Ringman, wearing the black crepe of the mourner and introducing the president of the Black Rapids Coal Company, is associated with Black Guinea in color—both in clear contrast with the deaf-mute in white and gold. The man in gray coat and white tie, arguing in behalf of the Negro cripple, insists that "the devil is never so black as he is painted" (p. 39). The dusk giant calls the herb-doctor "Snake!" (p. 94), and Pitch tells the herb-doctor that he is "the moderate man, the invaluable understrapper of the wicked man" (p. 119). The Intelligence Agent, speaking for the goodness of mature human nature in comparison with mischievous youth, asks Pitch, "Would you visit upon the butterfly the sins of the caterpillar?" As if describing the confidence man himself, Pitch answers: "The butterfly is the caterpillar in a gaudy cloak; stripped of which, there lies the impostor's long spindle of a body, pretty much worm-shaped as before" (pp. 131–32). The Intelligence Agent goes ashore at the "grotesquely-shaped bluff" called Devil's Joke (p. 136). Pitch only then realizes that "the insinuator's undulating flunkyisms dovetail into those of the flunky beast that windeth his way on his belly" (p. 138).

When the cosmopolitan appears in a confusion of colors, Pitch describes him as a toucan fowl with "fine feathers on foul meat" (p. 138). The cosmopolitan calls himself "a taster of races," who smacks his lips over "this racy creature, man," in all his vintages (p. 140). "Life is a pic-nic *en costume*," he asserts; "one must take a part, assume a character, stand ready in a sensible way to play the fool" (p. 141). And he is indeed the ultimate joke this April Fools' Day aboard the *Fidèle*. At midnight he puts out the solar lamp that brings total darkness to the "ship of fools." The author then concludes the narrative with this enigmatic sentence: "Something further may follow of this Masquerade" (p. 260). The ambiguity of the ending has led some critics to surmise that Melville intended to write a sequel to his tale. A more obvious meaning, though, would seem to be that Melville was suggesting *actual* apocalypse, the real end to the so-called American dream.

The Puritan preachers of the second and third generations used the day of doom to call the colonists back to fidelity to their covenant. Apocalyptic references were crucial to their indictment of declension. Yet it is Cotton Mather's *Magnalia Christi Americana*, oddly enough, that may give us a clearer understanding of the way that Melville was reading America at the time and why apocalypse was on his mind. There is reasonable assurance that Melville was familiar with this major Puritan text, reprinted in 1853. In addition to a possible allusion to it in "The Lightning-Rod Man" (1854), the *Magnalia* is mentioned explicitly in his story "The Apple-Tree Table," published in 1856 while Melville was working on *The Confidence-Man*. Chapter Five of the Seventh Book of the *Magnalia* is entitled "Wolves in Sheeps' Clothing: or, An History of Several Imposters, Pretending to be Ministers, Remarkably Detected in the Churches of New-England, With a Faithful Advice to All the Churches, Emitted by Some of the Pastors on That Occasion."[25] Mather laments the fact that no sure way has yet been found to keep impostors out of pulpits, despite the fact that the country since its first days has been plagued with them. That one Lyford, the first minister to come into the country, was an impostor is "an intimation from Heaven unto the country, to beware of all after-times how they suffered *cheats* in the evangelical ministry to be imposed upon them."[26] Getting down to theological considerations, Mather attributes man's fascination with false doctrine to a demonic drive of his mind, evidence no doubt of innate depravity:

> Fascination is a thing whereof mankind has more *experience* than *comprehension*; and fascination is never more notoriously sensible, than in man's running after *false teachers* of religion. When false teachers imposed on the Galatians, the apostle said, "O, foolish Galatians, who hath bewitched you!" One cannot easily ascribe unto a truer cause, than a *Satanick energy*, the strange *biass* upon the minds of the multitude, forceably and furiously sometimes carrying them into follies, from whence the plainest reason in the world will not reclaim them.[27]

In Melville's novel almost everyone is duped by false doctrine. The few who are not are either isolated from humanity by their self-reliance or already peddlers of false confidence. In Melville's imagination, though, the Puritan belief in innate depravity has come around full circle; the false teaching that depraved men are fascinated with is a naive optimism about the human potential.

In *The Confidence-Man*, Melville works almost exclusively within the apocalyptic symbolism of warning. Through the multiple disguises of the confidence man he introduces into American literature the secular analogue of the last loosing of Satan. In place of the individual Satan of the Bible, however, we have a variety of American types presented as the disguises of a single demonic con man, each duping the public with his own version of the plea for trust. The end imagined by Melville is the quiet darkness that ultimately shrouds the gentlemen's cabin. It is the cosmopolitan, the final disguise of the secular Satan, who extinguishes the last light that glimmers in America. The practicability of Christian charity is under scrutiny in Melville's work; judgment is woven subtly into the fabric of the confidence man's disguises. As he makes his way among the passengers of the *Fidèle*, he is able with his facile version of Christian teaching to dupe practically everyone into the acceptance of his false trust. If they are immune to his protestations, it is because they have already connived with evil themselves. The structural sequence of seven disguises symbolizes the completion of modern man's charade. Indeed, if Melville does not say that the darkness is final, the implication is that time ends after the seventh manifestation of the confidence man.

III

Getting to the meaning of Twain's *The Mysterious Stranger* has been complicated particularly by the confusion surrounding its curious final chapter.[28] As a result, the criticism of this posthumous publication has been too narrowly concerned with a "thematic" justification of the apparently inappropriate ending. Is there any preparation, the critics ask, for the utter negation of external reality that Philip Traum's revelation in the last chapter represents? Edwin Fussell finds a coherent development in the work to its solipsistic conclusion; it represents, he says, an objectification of the mental process whereby Theodor discards his mistaken belief in the reality of the world for an acceptance of the reality of dreams alone.[29] Pascal Covici thinks that "the most salient feature of *The Mysterious Stranger* is that Theodor's point of view changes and changes radically."[30] William C. Spengemann, seeing this last major work of Twain's in relation to *Tom Sawyer* and *Huckleberry Finn*, believes that the final chapter can be taken as the "logical conclusion" of the events which precede it if it is interpreted in terms of "escape from life in cosmic innocence."[31]

The excellence of these studies is nonetheless marred by the fact that the excessive concern for justifying the final chapter has forced them to be selective. They concentrate on the thematic development of the novel and thereby ignore much of the richness and coherence of the narrative structure. Any satisfactory treatment of the unity of the story must go beyond the thematic development to show, if possible, how the whole narrative contributes to the development of the discerned underlying theme. Coleman O. Parsons is credited with making the connection between the portrayal of Satan in the novel and the Jesus of the New Testament Apocrypha; there are clear references in Mark Twain's notebooks to the impression that the discovery of the apocryphal Gospels made upon him.[32] His indebtedness to the New Testament, however, whether conscious or unconscious, goes beyond the similarity of characterization. For if there is any principle of structural unity in *The Mysterious Stranger*, it is a variation of the Gospel form, which frequently—as in Matthew—juxtaposes the actions and discourses of Jesus within the pattern of his ministry of salvation. Moreover, action and discourse in the story are expanded in time and space, as we shall see, so that its progressively negative message becomes apocalyptic in scope. Although a Gospel in form, *The Mysterious Stranger* is anything but good news, because it announces not the celebration of reality but its annihilation.

The structural unity of *The Mysterious Stranger* develops out of Philip Traum's mission of salvation to Theodor Fischer. The narrative context of this process of education is circumscribed by Traum's three attempts to help Father Peter and his household—first, by giving Father Peter money to pay his debts; then, by helping Ursula and Marget while Father Peter is in jail; and finally, by possessing Wilhelm Meidling during his defense of Father Peter at the trial. A moral lesson, presented in the form of a discourse, is drawn from the circumstances surrounding each of these actions—which is rendered universal for Theodor's instruction by Traum's manipulation of time and space. It can be demonstrated that all of the narrative lies within this threefold framework, either as descriptive preparation for or dramatic consequence of the action taken, or as illustrative of Satan's discourses. For the purpose of describing the three segments of the story, if seems advisable to consider the whole novel, first, on the level of action and discourse, and only then to treat the significance of the threefold excursion into time and space. Although the summary of the narrative that follows may appear to be needlessly long, there is clearly no other way of demonstrating the underlying apocalyptic structure.

The narrative is set in a dreamy Austrian village in 1590. Austria itself was asleep, we are told; and Eseldorf "was in the middle of that sleep, being in the middle of Austria. . . . It was still the Middle Ages in Austria, and promised to remain so forever."[33] The medieval atmosphere of the village is accentuated as the narrator describes successively the castle, the absent prince, the importance of Christian training, the two priests, the astrologer, and the "inquisition."

The finely sketched introduction quickly reveals the situation out of which the three narrative strands will develop. Father Peter has been charged "with talking around in conversation that God was all goodness and would find a way to save all of his poor human children" (p. 163). The astrologer, Father Peter's open enemy and "a very powerful one" (p. 163)—because he impressed the bishop with his piety—was suspected of reporting Father Peter's statement to the bishop. Despite pleas for mercy from the priest's niece, Marget, the bishop "suspended Father Peter indefinitely" (pp. 163–64). For two years Father Peter has been without his flock, and he and his niece are in serious financial difficulty.

The way is prepared for the appearance of a savior. The morning after a nocturnal encounter with a ghost at the castle, Theodor Fischer and his inseparable companions, Seppi Wohlmeyer and Nikolaus Bauman, are talking over the experiences of the previous evening, in the shade of a nearby woody hilltop, when a youth comes strolling toward them through the trees. The handsome stranger tries to put the boys at ease by mirac-

ulously providing the fire that they need to be able to
smoke. He says that his name is Satan, even though he is
really Satan's nephew, an unfallen angel. When he is
trying to conceal his identity, he uses the name Philip
Traum.

Satan quickly commands the attention and interest
of the boys by creating some tiny people whom he later
wantonly destroys because they begin to argue and fight.
Satan's powers both charm and frighten the boys. They
are charmed by his creative ingenuity, yet appalled by
his merciless destruction of the people he has created.
From a narrative viewpoint, this passage serves the purpose of establishing his credentials as one who can achieve
the miraculous; it also provides the opportunity for
Satan to introduce the theme of his first discourse: that
man is the victim of the moral sense—"a sense whose
function is to distinguish between right and wrong,
with liberty to choose which of them he will do." "He is
always choosing," Satan insists, "and in nine cases out
of ten he prefers the wrong" (p. 193). This theme will
be developed throughout the first phase of the narrative,
which is concerned with the events resulting from
Satan's gift to Father Peter.

Thus, when Father Peter recovers his lost wallet in the
presence of the boys and finds it filled with money, the
boys know immediately the source of the money—even
though they cannot tell because Satan will not allow
them to reveal his identity. They nevertheless persuade
Father Peter to keep the money and use it to pay his
debts, until the rightful owner can be found.

The people attribute his good fortune to "the plain

hand of Providence." The ironic interplay of reality and belief is humorously suggested when one or two of the citizens say privately that "it looked more like the hand of Satan," and Theodor observes that "really that seemed a surprisingly good guess for ignorant people like that" (p. 180). Celebrating Father Peter's good fortune, the boys approach him to ask what the moral sense is. Father Peter's answer that "it is the one thing that lifts man above the beasts that perish and makes him heir to immortality" leaves the boys "filled but not fatted" (p. 181).

Father Peter's prosperity is short-lived, though. Accussed by the astrologer of stealing his money, Father Peter is put in jail; and his niece and the household are again reduced to penury. Concerned about Father Peter, Theodor thinks that he would like to see the jail; and he and Satan are there the next moment because Satan reads his thought. A young man accused of heresy is being tortured on a rack, and Theodor calls it "a brutal thing." Satan's response is a further elaboration on the perversity of the moral sense. "No, it was a human thing," he reminds Theodor; "you should not insult the brutes by such a misuse of that word. . . . No brute ever does a cruel thing—that is the monopoly of those with the Moral Sense" (p. 192). As a further illustration of the point, Satan takes Theodor to a French factory "where men and women and little children were toiling in heat and dirt and a fog of dust" (p. 193). Satan explains: "It is the Moral Sense which teaches the factory proprietors the difference between right and wrong— you perceive the result" (p. 194). The next moment

they are back on the streets of Eseldorf and hearing from
Seppi about the mysterious disappearance of Hans
Oppert, who has not been seen since he "brutally" struck
his faithful dog and knocked out one of his eyes. Satan
reminds them that "brutes do not act like that, but only
men" (p. 195). His lesson concerning the moral sense is
ironically heightened by the fact that the dog, despite
his beatings, has been trying in vain to direct the villagers to his dying master; but no one pays any attention
to the dog, and Hans dies without absolution.

At this point in the narrative the second strand has
already been introduced, because as soon as Father Peter
is imprisoned, Satan helps his household again by giving
Ursula, Father Peter's servant, the Lucky Cat—whose
owner "finds four silver groschen in his pocket every
morning" (p. 188). Human nature being what it is,
Ursula hires young Gottfried Narr to help around the
house—now that there is an abundance of money. The
boys wonder, though, about the wisdom of this decision
because Gottfried's grandmother had been burned as a
witch, and "the witch-terror had risen higher during
the past year than it had ever reached in the memory
of the oldest villagers" (p. 198). Theodor tells Satan
about Gottfried's grandmother and about eleven school-
girls all of whom had been forced by the commission
under duress to confess to witchcraft. Satan answers by
calling a bullock out of a pasture and emphasizing the
fact that animals, like angels, do not have the moral
sense and therefore "wouldn't drive children mad with
hunger and fright and loneliness," nor would they

"break the hearts of innocent, poor old women" (p. 200).

Again Providence was "getting all the gratitude" (p. 202) for the temporary well-being of Father Peter's household. But Father Adolf and the astrologer begin to suspect witchcraft, especially after Gottfried's remark in the presence of the latter that Marget and Ursula were living "on the fat of the land" (p. 201). When other means of detecting witchcraft have failed, they decide that they will use the party Marget has announced as an opportunity to discover with certainty the source of the household's abundance. When they see the house filled with delicacies, knowing that no supplies were brought in all week, they are convinced that it is "witchcraft . . . of a new kind—a kind never dreamed of before" (p. 204). Satan intervenes, though, to cast suspicion back on the astrologer and Father Adolf. The situation deteriorates when the possessed astrologer performs stunts in the market square beyond his age and powers. So rampant now is the fear of witchcraft that the townspeople are convinced that God has forsaken them.

These events lead directly into Satan's second discourse. Theodor feels that he has to try to reform Satan and begs him "to be more considerate and stop making people unhappy" (p. 210). They are in China at the time, and Satan explains to Theodor that there is nothing that can be done about the happiness quotient in a human's life. "Every man is a suffering-machine and a happiness-machine combined" (p. 211); and either happiness and suffering are equally divided, or suffering predominates. The principal point of this discourse and of the events that follow it by way of illustration through chapter 8 seems to be that there is so much necessary misery in human life that death comes as a genuine favor to victimized humanity. The determinism that is preached here does not, as some critics have suggested, imply a denial of the freedom that is necessary to make the perversity of man's moral sense deliberate; it is rather a determination to misery. If there is any lack of freedom, it is not the freedom of moral choice, but rather the freedom to choose happiness over misery. As a corollary to his instruction concerning the mercy of death in the light of human misery, Satan anticipates his ultimate denial of the reality of an afterlife, by denying the existence of purgatory and implying that there is no heaven.

The whole discussion of the inexorable sequence of man's acts—like the toppling of bricks laid in a row—is placed within the context of man's inability to know good fortune from bad because he cannot see into the future, where there is nothing but misery. Man's "first childish act" (p. 215), which situates him in particular circumstances, in a certain environment, can hardly be important from a moral point of view; it is simply the origin of his misery because it is the beginning of a life that only death can happily terminate. Satan, who can see all the possible careers open to an individual, knows that the only favor that can be done for a human being is either to terminate his life or to make him insane. The subsequent events in this second strand illustrate the mercy of death; in the third strand of the narrative, Satan will resort to insanity as salvation for Father Peter.

The conclusion of the second part of the story deals in some detail with the changes that Satan effects in the lives of Nikolaus, Frau Brandt, and Fischer the weaver. Of the three, only Fischer's life is lengthened; the defect in the change is the terrifying implication for Theodor that as a result of his new career Fischer will go to hell. Finally, the vision of human history from its beginning into the future, with no one but a "parcel of usurping little monarchs and nobilities" (p. 234) profiting from life, fortifies the lesson of human misery.

The third strand of the narrative focuses on the trial: Satan's victory for Father Peter through the defense by Wilhelm Meidling and the doctrine of laughter that Satan preaches as the only enduring antidote to the absurdities of life. The witch-commission, at first, is afraid to proceed against Father Peter and the astrologer —no doubt because of the esteem they are held in by the village. Instead they hang a poor, friendless lady, while a mob throws stones at her. Satan bursts out laughing, and his laughter is clearly significant. The crowd demands to know why he laughed and especially why he threw no stone. After answering his three accusers with the announcement of their imminent deaths, Satan admits to Theodor that he was actually laughing at him for throwing stones while his "heart revolted at the act" (p. 238). Distrust of neighbor and fear of reprisals had led the mob to be ruled by the malicious few.

When Father Peter eventually comes to trial, Satan possesses Wilhelm and, by demonstrating from the date on the coins that they could not belong to the astrologer, wins Father Peter's freedom. But the happiness that he had promised Theodor he would gain for Father Peter is the happiness of insanity; for he lies to Father Peter and tells him that he has been found guilty and been disgraced—and the shock dislodges the old man's reason. When Theodor reproaches Satan for his lie, Satan explains his action: "Are you so unobservant as not to have found out that sanity and happiness are an impossible combination? No sane man can be happy, for to him life is real, and he sees what a fearful thing it is. Only the mad can be happy, and not many of those" (p. 246).

Satan's third discourse follows immediately; it is an explanation of his laughter during the stoning episode as well as a corollary to his observations on insanity and happiness. The human race, he insists, lacks a genuine sense of humor. They see "the comic side of a thousand low-grade and trivial . . . incongruities"—another example of the "continuous and uninterrupted self-deception" that enslaves the race, but they miss thereby "the ten-thousand high-grade comicalities which exist in the world." The only antidote to these radical inconsistencies is to "laugh at them—and by laughing at them destroy them." He concludes: "Against the assault of laughter nothing can stand" (pp. 247–48). We understand now the curious rationality behind his salvation of Father Peter. Both laughter and insanity negate reality; but since the race lacks the courage to laugh, insanity was the only sure redemption for Father Peter.

The excursion to India is the last narrative episode of the novel; and although it seems somehow unequal to its climactic position in the narrative, it does nevertheless serve as a summary illustration of Satan's gospel. The foreigner, a Portuguese colonist, refuses to allow the natives to enjoy the fruit of Satan's tree even for an hour because the tree is on his property. The natives respond with humble obeisance to their master. Only the moral sense can explain the foreigner's perversity, and the misery of the groveling natives is another example of the foolish acceptance of the master-slave relationship "which is the foundation upon which all civilizations have been built" (p. 234). The foreigner will conceal his acceptance of the sentence Satan has imposed upon him—for fear of the natives. Only by preventing their revenge can he secure his ascendancy over them. The "high-grade" incongruity of the foreigner's situation is that he will "fetch a priest to cast out the tree's devil" (p. 250). Of course, the priest's incantations will be ineffectual; such belief itself is the ultimate incongruity of the race because it is patently groundless.

Before discussing the final chapter in relationship to the narrative as it has unfolded thus far, we must consider the cosmic dimension added to the narrative structure by the threefold excursion into time and space. "It was wonderful," Theodor exclaims at the beginning of chapter 9, "the mastery Satan had over time and distance" (p. 235). An overview of Twain's method of universalizing the lessons learned through the process of Father Peter's salvation is crucial to a proper understaning of the apocalyptic position of the controversial last chapter.

Each of Satan's three discourses is applied to all of

humanity—in space and in time. In the first strand, the
journey to the French factory becomes a spatial confirmation of the universal perversity of man's moral sense.
The temporal expansion of the discourse is achieved by
Satan's symbolic repetition of the creation of the world.
The sequence of miracles by which he establishes his
angelic powers (which are really more divine than angelic, according to any traditional theological model)—
fire, ice, fruit, animals, and finally men—corresponds
roughly to the order of creation found in the first chap-
te of Genesis—light, firmament, plants, animals, and
man. There would seem to be no other reason for this
succession of miracles, in precisely this order, than to
take us back in time to the very origin of man's problem
—his creation as a being endowed with the moral sense.

The setting of the second discourse is China, as far
removed from Eseldorf as is spatially conceivable on this
planet. We may conjecture that the reason "why Satan
chose China for this excursion instead of another place"
(p. 210) is that he has thereby encircled the globe with
his doctrine of necessary human misery, determined by
the very fact of our existence in this world. The temporal excursion during this portion encompasses the
whole of human history from Cain through the present
and then "two or three centuries" into the future of the
race, exhibiting only "a mighty procession" (p. 234) of
slaughter and oppression.

The third discourse deals with laughter's capacity to
annul the appalling incongruities of reality. The last
spatial excursion is to India and Ceylon; and the episode
which occurs is, as we have seen, weakly illustrative of

Philip Traum's total vision of the human race. The location, though, suggests that Twain was thinking consciously of *maya*, the Hindu belief in man's capacity to laugh at the illusory nature of all reality, as a prelude to the final encounter between Theodor and Satan. The last chapter with its announcement of the dream quality of reality becomes the temporal conclusion to the story. To be fully understood within the structure of the work, it must be seen—in juxtaposition to creation at the beginning of the narrative—as the apocalypse of the end of time. We can see now more clearly too the progression from insanity through laughter to dream—since the proclamation that all reality is nothing but a dream is, of course, the theoretical ultimate in this series of views destructive of reality.

Understood as apocalypse, the final chapter both completes the temporal progression of the novel and helps us to comprehend the nature of the change that has come over Theodor, because there can be no doubt that there is a qualitative difference between his encounter with Satan in the last chapter and their relationship until then. If we trace the development of Theodor's attitude toward Satan through the three stages of the narrative, we find that he moves from a period of profound shock at Satan's indifference to humanity, to a desire to reform Satan's ways, and finally to an attitude of diminished grief and private disapproval of Satan's actions. When Satan's lie has resulted in Father Peter's insanity, Theodor reflects: "Privately I did not think much of his processes" (p. 247). And after Satan's punishment of the Portuguese landowner, he admits that it grieved him, "though not sharply, to see [Satan] take such a malicious satisfaction in his plans" (p. 250) for the foreigner. There is no simple linear development in Theodor's acceptance of Satan's shocking vision of humanity.

The level of response that we have traced thus far is primarily concerned with Satan's attitude and the consequent harshness of his actions. Running throughout the story, though, is the far more important motif of the boys' personal attachment to Philip. The enchantment of the person—the lure of his music, the excitement of his presence, and the ecstasy of his wine from heaven—is pronounced from the beginning and only grows in intensity as the story unfolds. "He made us drunk with the joy of being with him, and of looking into the heaven of his eyes, and of feeling the ecstasy that thrilled our veins from the touch of his hand" (p. 171). It is undoubtedly this attachment to the power of Philip's personality that becomes the ground for Theodor's leap of faith in accepting his final revelation.

But Satan himself is a dream and nothing more. How are we to understand this subtler aspect of the final revelation? "I am but a dream—your dream, creature of your imagination. . . . I, your poor servant, have revealed you to yourself and set you free. Dream other dreams, and better!" (p. 252). The dream that has uttered a final and definitive "No!" to reality is a dream that is conditioned by the age of belief—and which denies the reality of God, heaven, hell, the human race, and the universe. What is rejected here by Theodor's imagination is quite simply but emphatically a Christian explanation of existence. But it is also more than this. It is a rejection of any reality outside of the self. Theodor is nothing more than "a vagrant thought, . . . wandering forlorn among the empty eternities!" (p. 253). The only better dream, then, that he can presumably dream is laughter.

We are left, finally, with the problem of the apparent incongruity of an *adolescent* narrator who is a solipsist. However, even though the first person point of view is used, the story is narrated in the past tense—which indicates the passage of time between the actual occurrence of the events and the time of narration. Despite the fact that an effort is made to maintain the youthful point of view, there are certain passages where the age of the narrator shows through. In the opening paragraph, the narrator indicates that the Austria of the story is a remembrance, but that he remembers it well even though he was "only a boy" (p. 161). In recalling his last days with Nick, he notes: "It was an awful eleven days; and yet, with a lifetime stretching back between today and then, they are still a grateful memory to me, and beautiful" (p. 222). In chapter 10, while commenting on the fact that Satan seemed to know of no other way to do a person a favor except "by killing him or making a lunatic out of him," he adds: "Privately, I did not think much of his processes—*at that time*" (p. 247, my emphasis). And during Satan's final revelation, there is the patently adult exclamation: "By God! I had had that very thought a thousand times in my musings" (p. 252). Rather than consider these as lapses from the established viewpoint, as some critics have done, it seems more reasonable to explain them as intended emphasis of the passage of time. It certainly makes it easier for us to understand and accept the final vision of reality if we realize that it is an old man who is reflecting the bitterness of age, or at least a process of many years.

The paradox of Twain's brief apocalypse is that the Satan he has loosed in Eseldorf is supposed to be a savior of men, not a destroyer. More accurately, the Satan of *The Mysterious Stranger* is to save Theodor by destroying his Christian vision of the world. The world is not literally destroyed by catastrophe; its reality, however, is dissolved by demonic fiat. What is judged totally inadequate to explain the misery of the world is apparently the *Weltanschauung* of Twain's Presbyterian heritage. Twain uses the Gospel form for reverse effect. His savior does not give life more abundantly; he reduces reality to a solipsistic minimum.

Twain uses the apocalyptic motif of the loosed Satan to pass judgment on what he considers to be the absurdity of Christianity—the belief in human freedom, the expectation of happiness, and the absence of a radical sense of humor. Since by hypothesis the Satan of the story is a figment of Theodor's imagination, Theodor has in effect convinced himself that there is no reality outside of himself. The realization is final. The only new life is paradoxically the denial of any life outside of the self. And the way of *maya* is presumably the only better dream—to laugh amid the miseries of existence because all is illusion.

As was noted earlier, Cotton Mather saw intimations of continuing American fascination with false doctrine in the accepted chicanery of the first minister; however, he offered the consolation of an orthodox faith and the continuing presence of theological observers to point out falsehood and its perpetrators. Hawthorne, in *The Blithedale Romance*, holds open the possibility of striving for the ideal, but only within the real order of "care and sorrow, and troubled joy." Melville's only orthodoxy in *The Confidence-Man* seems to be the impossibility of achieving the ideal as embodied in Christianity. It is too good to be true. In a world overrun with impostors, facile confidence and inhuman self-reliance are the only options; they are equally apocalyptic because they lead inevitably to disaster. And Twain in *The Mysterious Stranger*, overwhelmed by the misery of human existence, denies the reality of the world created by religious belief in an apocalypse of solipsistic laughter.

CHAPTER THREE

Words and Deeds:

Apocalyptic Judgment in Faulkner, West, and O'Connor

In his introduction to *Everything That Rises Must Converge*, Robert Fitzgerald recalls that he owed his first reading of both *Miss Lonelyhearts* and *As I Lay Dying* to Flannery O'Connor's insistence. He goes on to add: "These are the only two works of fiction that I can remember her urging on me, and it is pretty clear from her work that they were close to her heart as a writer."[1] There are striking similarities between *As I Lay Dying* and Flannery O'Connor's novel *The Violent Bear It Away*; *Miss Lonelyhearts*, although revealing definite thematic parallels to *The Violent Bear It Away*, seems more closely related in imaginative intensity to her shorter fiction. My purpose here, however, is not to demonstrate Flannery O'Connor's literary indebtedness to William Faulkner and Nathanael West. Where relationships among the three novels are pointed out, they will hopefully support my exposition of the workings of the apocalyptic imagination in these extraordinarily powerful twentieth-century novels.

I

In Faulkner's *As I Lay Dying*, the images and narrative developments associated with Addie's death and burial are, in their public or cosmic dimension, types of the primitive religious symbolism of chaos. There is the even more significant private dimension of these images in which the chaos of Addie's death becomes the source of personal revelation and judgment, and ultimately of new life—the fullness of Christian apocalyptic imagery. In speaking of death as revelation, I refer specifically to Peabody's seemingly normative assessment of death's meaning: "When I was young I believed death to be a phenomenon of the body; now I know it to be merely a function of the mind—and that of the minds of the ones who suffer the bereavement. The nihilists say it is the end; the fundamentalists, the beginning; when in reality it is no more than a single tenant or family moving out of a tenement or a town."[2] Excluding both beginning and end from consideration, Peabody helps us to focus on the temporal effect of death. And even though his elaboration of the temporal is minimal, he has done us the service of redirecting our attention. The novel itself will add the corrective notion of temporal development to his perspective of displacement.

Michael Millgate has observed that the simple narrative of *As I Lay Dying* "is deliberately presented as being played out against the background of cosmic scale."[3] He goes on to say: "Mood and setting are continually evoked on this grandiose scale, and there is a persistent invocation, in the description and in the imagery, of the elements of earth, air, fire and water."[4] Although Millgate's observation is perceptive, it lacks focus because he has failed both to distinguish the levels of emphasis in the cosmic imagery and to discover a significant reason for such a "grandiose scale."

It is quite true that each of the four primary elements figures prominently in the imagery of the novel. Dewey Dell, unmistakably allied with the earth, seems most sensitive to air as well. She feels the breathing of the cow through her dress: "She nuzzles at me, snuffing, blowing her breath in a sweet, hot blast, through my dress, against my hot nakedness, moaning" (p. 59). The cow wants to be milked, but the disturbed Dewey Dell can think only of her own unwanted pregnancy. Again she reflects on the cow's breath: "Then the dead, hot, pale air breathes on my face again. . . . The dead air shapes the dead earth in the dead darkness, further away than seeing shapes the dead earth. It lies dead and warm upon me, touching me naked through my clothes" (p. 61). She is so preoccupied with the child growing inside her that she considers herself "a wet seed wild in the hot blind earth" (p. 61). She is alone because Lafe has left, and she knows that "the process of coming unalone is terrible" (p. 59). The breath of the cow that touches her body in the darkness is the sole, ironical violation of her aloneness.

Despite these pointed references to air and earth, water and fire undoubtedly dominate the imagery of the novel. And water and fire are primary images in the apocalyptic symbolism of chaos. They are traditional religious images for the initiatory passage through chaos that precedes the dawn of the new year, the rebirth of man, the advent of wisdom. Water and fire are also classic Christian symbols related to the purifying process of initiation and judgment. Matthew and Luke associate the images with John the Baptist: "I baptize you with water, for repentance; but the one who comes after me is mightier than I. . . . He will baptize you with the Holy Spirit and with fire."[5]

It is Addie's assertion that Jewel "will save [her] from the water and the fire" (p. 160) that elevates to the level of symbol the fording of the Yoknapatawpha and the burning of Gillespie's barn. Water literally dominates the first part of the narrative, as fire does the latter. The very evening that the narrative begins, "it's fixing to rain" (p. 33). The gathering storm both looks like sulphur and smells like it; air becomes a function of water and fire. When Darl and Jewel leave to make their delivery, "the sun, an hour above the horizon, is poised like a bloody egg upon a crest of thunderheads; the light has turned copper: in the eye portentous, in the nose sulphurous, smelling of lightning" (p. 39). Anse sees the road as bad luck that brings rain to his house and cuts him off from his sons and the team that he needs to bring Addie back to Jefferson: "And now I can see same as second sight the rain shutting down betwixt us, a-coming up that road like a durn man, like it want ere a other house to rain on in all the living land" (p. 36). As Peabody is being hauled up to the house, the daylight

that remains is "the color of sulphur matches" (p. 42).
Darl imagines that "they will haul him up the path,
balloon-like up the sulphurous air" (p. 39).

Just before the storm, the atmosphere is so heavy with
the smell of sulphur that the shadows of Cash and Anse
seem to form on it "as upon a wall." Then, "it begins
to rain. The first harsh, sparse, swift drops rush through
the leaves and across the ground in a long sigh, as though
of relief from intolerable suspense. They are big as buck-
shot, warm as though fired from a gun; they sweep
across the lantern in a vicious hissing" (p. 72). Later,
when Vardaman reaches the Tulls with the news of
Addie's death, he looks "like a drowned puppy, in them
overalls, without no hat, splashed up to his knees where
he had walked them four miles in the mud" (p. 66).
When Whitfield arrives, "he is wet and muddy to the
waist" (p. 83). He has after all crossed the flooding
river safely—"the travail by water," he reflects, "which
I sustained by the strength of His hand" (p. 171).

The three days that they wait for Darl and Jewel to
return are enough for the storm to take its toll on the
land, swelling the river and creeks and washing away the
bridges, so that the only way to Jefferson is by fording
the river. "The thick dark current" (p. 134) of the river
runs before them. It was as though they "had reached the
place where the motion of the wasted world accelerates
just before the final precipice" (p. 139). The swollen
river is a "surging and heaving desolation" (p. 141).
The despair in the mules' eyes indicates that "they had
already seen in the thick water the shape of the disaster
which they could not speak" (p. 139). The fording of

the river, as grotesquely dramatic as it is, is by no means the end of the water's influence on the journey. Addie may have been hauled ashore, but Cash's tools have been lost and must be retrieved; his broken leg is attended to, however inadequately; and Addie's soaked body becomes an even more appealing prey to vultures.

Addie's body is a physical link between the water and the fire. The fact that "she talks in little trickling bursts of secret and murmurous bubbling" (p. 202) under the apple tree at Gillespie's—suggesting the bloated condition of her body—seems to be the principal reason why Darl decides to end the journey by fire. Once the barn is ablaze, Darl remains a passive witness in the effort to rescue Addie. He observes that "the sound of [the fire] has become quite peaceful now, like the sound of the river did" (p. 211). As in the passage through water, the effects of the fire remain with the family. Jewel's back is black from burns, and Anse has Darl committed to an asylum in Jackson rather than accept responsibility for the damage to Gillespie's barn.

Narrative developments related to the symbolism of chaos all belong to the genre of grotesque humor that is considered typically Southern. Addie's death lays bare the absurd disorder of the Bundren family. It takes her ten days to die; and during this whole period, she silently supervises the construction of her coffin, "lying there with her head propped up so she could watch Cash building the coffin" (p. 22). Her body makes "no more of a hump than a rail would, and the only way you can tell she is breathing is by the sound of the mattress shucks" (p. 8). Passers-by comment on Cash's fine carpentry, so that Jewel feels that "every bastard in the country [is] coming in to stare at her" (p. 15).

After Addie dies, while Anse is watching Cash finish the coffin in the rain, the water streaming down Anse's face looks "as though upon a face carved by a savage caricaturist, a monstrous burlesque of all bereavement flowed" (pp. 73–74). Vardaman, convinced that Peabody "came and did it" (p. 52) simply because Addie dies *after* his arrival, lets the doctor's team go in a cloud of dust. The bereaved Vardaman tries twice to revive his dead mother with fresh air and succeeds only in letting the rain in on her body through the open window. When the coffin is finished, "they put her into it and nailed it down so he couldn't open the window on her no more" (p. 69). Not to be outdone, Vardaman bores holes in the top of the box, and "two of them had bored on into her face" (p. 70). Cash meticulously fills the holes in the coffin lid, but the only way they can repair Addie is to make her "a veil out of a mosquito bar so the auger holes in her face wouldn't show" (p. 83).

Addie is laid out head to foot in the coffin because of the flared bottom on her wedding dress. There is of course ironic humor, although no doubt folk tradition as well, in Addie's being buried in her wedding dress, since her marriage to Anse is what has, colloquially speaking, "laid her out." The coffin's initial resistance to being lifted is considered an effect of Addie's enduring modesty: "For an instant it resists, as though volitional, as though within it her pole-thin body clings furiously, even though dead, to a sort of modesty, as she would have tried to conceal a soiled garment that she could not prevent her body soiling. Then it breaks free, rising suddenly as though the emaciation of her body had added buoyancy to the planks or as though, seeing that the garment was about to be torn from her, she rushes suddenly after it in a passionate reversal that flouts its own desire and need" (pp. 91–92).

Because so much difficulty is in fact encountered in transporting the body to Jefferson, it would seem that having made the request of Anse, Addie herself oversees the humorous prolongation of her vengeful passage to a final resting place. When the coffin slips off the wagon in fording the swollen river, it is Vardaman's traumatized mind that records the ludicrous struggle: "Cash tried but she fell off and Darl jumped going under he went under . . . and Vernon passed me because he was seeing her come up and she jumped into the water again and Darl hadn't caught her yet . . . and I hollering catch her darl catch her darl because in the water she could go faster than a man and Darl had to grabble for her so I knew he could catch her because he is the best grabbler even with the mules in the way again they dived up rolling their feet stiff rolling down again and their backs up now . . ." (pp. 143–144). When the wagon is finally hauled ashore after the disastrous passage through the water, the coffin "lies profoundly" in the wagon bed, "the long pale planks hushed a little with wetting yet still yellow, like gold seen through water, save for two long muddy smears" (p. 150). Cash has broken his leg in the struggle, the same one that he broke in his fall from the church, and he lies on the shore, "a little pool of vomit at his head and a thread of it running from the corner of his mouth" (p. 149). Jewel and Vernon Tull risk the rampaging flood waters again in order to recover one by one the tools from Cash's box. "There was a shoat come by, blowed up like a balloon" (p. 148); and Anse's team drowns in the violent current.

Chaos in the mode of grotesque humor continues apace with the journey to Jefferson. The disabled Cash rides in incestuous discomfort "on top of Addie." He vomits again when they lay him down, "but he got his head over the wagon bed in time" (p. 172). Anse will permit no interruption of the already tortuously slow process of getting Addie buried, and so he immobilizes Cash's leg by pouring cement on it. When his foot and leg begin to turn black, they try to get the cement off but it simply cracks and adheres to his leg. Peabody finally sees the leg, and he tells Cash, but especially Anse, that the price for the cement cast will be that Cash will "have to limp around on one short leg" for the rest of his life, if he walks at all. Peabody bludgeons Cash with the absurdity of Anse's cheap remedy: "God Amighty, why didn't Anse carry you to the nearest sawmill and stick your leg in the saw? That would have cured it. Then you all could have stuck his head into the saw and cured the whole family" (p. 230).

The chorus of accompanying vultures and the neighborly notice given to the strength of the aging corpse are two particular motifs of grotesque humor that contribute to the pervasive sense of chaos. Darl describes the delicate process of carrying the coffin down to the waiting wagon; it is already three days since Addie's death: "We move, balancing it as though it were something

infinitely precious, our faces averted, breathing through
our teeth to keep our nostrils closed" (p. 92). When they
reach Mottson and stop to buy some cement, the ladies
are "all scattering up and down the street with handker-
chiefs to their noses." The druggist Moseley compares
the arrival of the body to "a piece of rotten cheese coming into an ant-hill" (p. 193). When Moseley goes home
for supper, "it still seemed like [he] could smell it"
(pp. 194–95). At Gillespie's they have to move Addie
from under the apple tree to the barn because "the
wind's changed" (p. 206). Entering Jefferson, they pass
three Negroes: "Their heads turn suddenly with that
expression of shock and instinctive outrage. 'Great God,'
one says; 'what they got in that wagon?'" (p. 219).
Jewel's ill-timed response to the Negro's exclamation
nearly involves him in a fight with a white man.

The omnipresent buzzards become a kind of grotesque
chorus to a mock-heroic drama. At first they are "no
more than specks, implacable, patient, portentous" (p.
88); they are already above the farm awaiting the return
of Darl and Jewel. Samson finds one in his barn after the
Bundrens have moved on: "I thought at first it was one
of them got left, then I saw what it was. It was a buzzard. It looked around and saw me and went on down
the hall, spraddle-legged, with its wings kind of hunk-
ered out, watching me first over one shoulder and then
over the other, like a old bald-headed man. When it got
out doors it begun to fly. It had to fly a long time before
it ever got up into the air, with it thick and heavy and
full of rain like it was" (p. 112). At Armstid's, Vardaman has to run one out of the barn; in fact, Armstid

reports that the boy was "chasing them buzzards all day in the hot sun until he was nigh as crazy as the rest of them" (p. 182).

The vultures are most frequently associated with the motionlessness which is a recurring image of the novel and seemingly the major characteristic of the Bundren journey. They "hang in soaring circles, the clouds giving them an illusion of retrograde" (p. 89). When the Bundrens approach New Hope for the second time, a solitary buzzard in the sky looks "as still as if he were nailed to it" (p. 116). Later Vardaman and Darl "watch them in little tall black circles of not-moving" (p. 185). Just outside of Jefferson, "they hang in narrowing circles, like the smoke, with an outward semblance of form and purpose, but with no inference of motion, progess or retrograde" (p. 216).

It is Vardaman's desire to "find where they stay at night" (p. 215) that leads him to discover Darl setting fire to the barn—as if to "get shut of her in some clean way" (p. 223), Cash is inclined to think later. The fire brings to a climax the grotesquery of the chaotic journey. In the light of the fire the doorway of the barn seems to be "broken only by the square squat shape of the coffin on the sawhorses like a cubistic bug" (p. 209). The coffin is actually inside the barn, so that Jewel, rescuing Addie alone after the livestock have been removed, must keep upending it so that it will topple forward to safety. Since he is Addie's favorite son, he too is allowed an incestuous ride on the coffin: "Without stopping it overends and rears again, pauses, then crashes slowly forward and through the curtain. This time Jewel is riding upon it, clinging to it, until it crashes down and flings him forward and clear" (p. 212). The thought of the condition of Addie's body as it reaches Jefferson overpowers the imagination, especially in view of the initial complication of their "not having a regular man to fix her and it being July and all" (p. 108). There must be some virtue, though, in reaching a destination against such odds, but what it is is obscured by the shadow of vultures and the smell of dead flesh nine summer days old. One has no difficulty agreeing with Cash that to save her from the flood "was going against God in a way" and that when Darl set fire to the barn "he done right in a way" (p. 223).

The basis for understanding the revelatory function of Addie's death and burial, as the focal point for the cosmic and narrative images of chaos, lies in the sole portion of the novel to be told from Addie's viewpoint. Significantly, this passage occurs *after* Addie's death to emphasize the fact that, even though dead, Addie still dominates the action of the novel through her body and controls the lives of family, friends, and even strangers.

Addie awakens to the realization that "words are no good; that words dont ever fit even what they are trying to say at" (p. 163). Words are invented by people who have to have words because they have never had the experience that the word goes with. Addie claims to have discovered this when Cash, her first child, was born; then she knew that motherhood was a word invented by someone who had never been a mother "because the ones that had the children didn't care whether there was a word for it or not" (p. 163). Love, like every

other word, is "just a shape to fill a lack" (p. 164).
Deeds alone count. Addie understands "how words go
straight up in a thin line, quick and harmless, and how
terribly doing goes along the the earth, clinging to it, so
that after a while the two lines are too far apart for the
same person to straddle from one to the other" (p. 165).
And so she would lie awake at night listening to "the
dark voicelessness in which the words are the deeds, and
the other words that are not deeds, that are just the gaps
in peoples' lacks, coming down like the cries of the geese
out of the wild darkness in the old terrible nights, fum-
bling at the deeds like orphans to whom are pointed out
in a crowd two faces and told, That is your father, your
mother" (p. 166).

If Addie first realizes the meaninglessness of words
when Cash is born, it is not until Darl is born that she
knows that she has been tricked by words older than
love or Anse. It is presumably the very cycle of life and
death that Addie has been tricked by, tricked into thinking that it would somehow truly "violate her aloneness."
So it was then that she decided that she would take
revenge on Anse: "And that my revenge would be that
he would never know that I was taking revenge" (p.
164). Since Anse is given to mouthing words about duty
and obligation, he will see her request as an expression
of her own filial piety. In asking Anse to take her back
to Jefferson, she knows that even if life has tricked her
into living with Anse, death will not trick her into being
buried with him. She thus acknowledges that her father
was right when he "used to say that the reason for living
was to get ready to stay dead a long time" (p. 161),

even though she feels that he could not have realized fully what he meant. Believing that she is getting ready to stay dead—a process that she calls "cleaning up the house" (p. 168)—she can also take revenge on Anse by sinning with Whitfield (and Anse would never know that either), thus preparing a child to save her from being with Anse in death. Jewel will bring her through water and fire to the promised land of her birth, the only salvation that she wants. For when "sin is just a matter of words, . . . salvation is just words too" (p. 168).

Participation in Addie's death and burial becomes a *rite de passage* for each of the Bundrens, revealing the level of maturity of each as they are tried in the crucible of Addie's voiceless world. Addie speaks of Anse having "three children that are his and not [hers]" (p. 168), and it would seem reasonable that they would be the three more addicted to words rather than deeds, in the likeness of Anse. Darl, Dewey Dell, and Vardaman actually contribute nothing to their mother's burial; they either impede the process or accompany the coffin for their own ulterior motives. That Jewel and Cash stand in a special relationship to Addie is clear not only from what they *do* in the course of the narrative, but also obviously from Addie's revelation of her predilection for them. Although Jewel is the one who literally saves Addie from water and fire, it is Cash who has constructed the vessel for her passage through chaos to dubious salvation. Jewel like Addie speaks only once, and Cash just five times; but three of the five passages devoted to him contain nothing more than technical observations about beveling and the balance of the coffin. Addie calls Jewel her "cross and salvation," a cross no doubt because she had to conceal her special love for him, her salvation because she conceived him in sin to save herself from Anse. About the love between herself and Cash, Addie says simply this: "Cash did not need to say it to me nor I to him" (p. 164). And this speaks volumes once we understand Addie's scorn for words.

Jewel clearly represents an extreme of voicelessness; and his mother's death reveals not only his capacity for action but also the reasons for it. Jewel is a man of strong passion who is unable to transcend the oedipal bond. The Snopes's horse is after all nothing but an ersatz mother. It had to be Jewel and his horse against the world since it could never be Jewel and Addie the way he had wanted. He fantasizes about his dying mother: "It would just be me and her on a high hill and me rolling the rocks down the hill at their faces, picking them up and throwing them down the hill faces and teeth and all by God until she was quiet and not that goddamn adze going One lick less" (p. 15). As they carry the coffin down to the waiting wagon, Darl senses the weight of it lifted from him "as though it coasts like a rushing straw upon the furious tide of Jewel's despair" (p. 92). As if making amends for delaying the funeral because he had misjudged her readiness to die, Jewel relentlessly executes her literal will to be transported physically to her family burying ground. Reluctantly, he allows Anse to sell his horse, but he alone delivers the horse to the Snopes's place just as he delivers his mother to Jefferson. The passage through water and fire reveals his physical courage, his impetuosity, his monomaniacal energy in the execution of his mother's revenge.

Cash's addiction to deeds is certainly less flamboyant than Jewel's, yet in his quiet way he reveals a level of mature devotion that extends beyond Addie to embrace the whole family. Cash is a "good carpenter" (p. 4); and as he saws "the long hot sad yellow days up into planks" (p. 25) for Addie's coffin—under her careful scrutiny—one can get the impression that this is all he is. The first three times that the narrative unfolds from his viewpoint (pp. 77, 90, 157), we are treated to the unimaginative reflections of a carpenter. He gives thirteen reasons why he "made it on the bevel." As if anticipating the difficulties of the journey, he notes as an advantage of beveling that "water moves easiest up and down or straight across" (p. 77). Addie wants the coffin made well, among other reasons no doubt because she is going "to stay dead a long time" (p. 161); and Cash is the man to do a precise job. He is so ludicrously precise he recalls that his fall from the church when he broke his leg was "twenty-eight foot, four and a half inches, about" (p. 85). He is methodical and thrifty enough to take his tools on the trip to Jefferson so that he can repair Vernon Tull's barn roof on the way back, without an extra trip. And when Anse takes the money that he has saved to buy "that talking machine" (p. 181), he is dutiful enough to relinquish it, apparently without resistance. Yet to speak only of Cash's mechanical piety is to ignore his profoundly humane appraisal of the family, in the last two portions of the narrative told from his viewpoint. The journey to Jefferson has revealed in him a capacity for growth and a level of awareness unrivaled in the family.

Dewey Dell lies somewhere in the middle of the spectrum that has words and deeds for its extremes. She is so alone in her fear of being discovered pregnant that her mother's death and burial are nothing but an opportunity for her to seek an abortion. Darl knows and he tells her: "You want her to die so you can get to town" (p. 38). She is never able to break out of the confinement of her own personal anxiety, to react either in word or deed to her mother's passing. Even when Peabody comes to preside over Addie's death, she can only brood over how "he could do so much for [her] if he just would" (p. 56). Moseley, the Mottson druggist, no doubt sees her precisely as "dumb and hopeful and sullenly willing to be disappointed" (p. 190). Her desire to come "unalone" through an abortion is so all-consuming that she allows herself stupidly to be taken advantage of again, this time by the clerk MacGowan and in the name of medicine. She hates Darl because of his special knowledge; and perhaps because she has imagined killing him (p. 115), she is able to be the first one to restrain him when the wardens come. Cash observes that "it was Dewey Dell that was on him before even Jewel could get at him" (p. 227).

What Vardaman *does* is unfortunately all counterproductive to the grotesque adventure that Addie's revenge sets in motion. Her death reveals a very sensitive child, who experiences severe emotional trauma because of it.[6] Next to Darl, Vardaman has the greatest number

of passages devoted to his viewpoint. Once we realize
that in his trauma Addie has literally become the fish
that he caught the day of her death, we can transpose
Vardaman's observations into fairly objective language.
In discussing the grotesque humor of the narrative, I
have already detailed Vardaman's efforts to free his
mother from the confinement of her coffin. During the
course of the journey, his disturbed imagination is
torn between a preoccupation with vultures and his
anticipation of eating bananas and seeing the toy train.

Darl and Anse would seem at first to win equal hon-
ors for saying rather than doing, but this could only be
because of Darl's apparent monopoly of the narrative.
Addie's death reveals Darl's capacity to pierce through
masks to the substance of relationships. He actually
seems at times to act as death's prophet, speaking out to
the concerned parties the truth that they have kept hidden. But in communicating his extraordinary knowledge, he is not necessarily bound to words. Dewey Dell,
speaking of her pregnancy, insists that Darl "said he
knew without the words" (p. 26). Vernon Tull reflects
in this way on the piercing quality of Darl's eyes: "It's
like he had got into the inside of you, someway. Like
somehow you was looking at yourself and your doings
outen his eyes" (p. 119). More often than not, Darl
flaunts his privileged knowledge at Jewel. The latter is
obviously the special object of his persecution because
it is Jewel's mother who has died, and Darl doubtlessly
harbors secret resentment of Jewel for replacing him in
his mother's affections. And so Darl persuades Jewel
to deliver another load of lumber, knowing that Addie

will die in their absence; then, from the distance of the road, he announces Addie's death (p. 51).

Anse believes in deeds, provided they are done for him. Otherwise his life is filled with incessant mindless chatter about promises, filial piety, and "not being beholden." His mature reflection on Addie's death is simply this: "God's will be done. . . . Now I can get them teeth" (p. 51). He has been waiting for fifteen years to "eat God's own victuals as a man should" (p. 36). He allows Darl and Jewel to leave on the eve of their mother's death because he needs the three dollars for his teeth. Later, when they have to purchase a new team, Anse takes Cash's graphophone money and Jewel's horse. His justification for selling the horse is a parody of familial equality: "I thought that if I could do without eating, my sons could do without riding. God knows I did" (p. 182). When finally he takes Dewey Dell's abortion money in order to get his teeth, a shave, and a new wife (apparently in that order of importance), it is quite clear that Anse can say "We would be beholden to no man" (p. 19) because it is easier for him and safer too to steal from his own children.

Anse "was beginning to hump" (p. 162) even when he was courting Addie; he is of course perfectly humped by the time of her funeral. The hump was not, obviously, the result of overwork. Darl says: "I have never seen a sweat stain on his shirt. He was sick once from working in the sun when he was twenty-two years old, and he tells people that if he ever sweats, he will die. I suppose he believes it" (pp. 16-17). Although Cora Tull's estimate of Addie seems consistently to miss the mark, Vernon is surely accurate when he says that "the only burden Anse Bundren's ever had is himself" (p. 70). Promising Anse help, Vernon observes: "Like most folks around here, I done holp him so much already I can't quit now" (p. 32). Armstid's comment on the continuing need to help Anse is that there is "something about a durn fellow like Anse that seems to make a man have to help him, even when he knows he'll be wanting to kick himself next minute" (p. 183).

Anse unconsciously becomes a living parody of the marital covenant. Insisting that there is no luck in turning back, he reminds his children: "I give my promise. . . . She is counting on it" (p. 133). It obviously is not love that motivates him, simply the compulsion to conceal *his* purpose behind the jargon of Christian duty. When Darl complains that they should have had someone prepare the grave for their arrival, Anse has the unmitigated nerve to tell them all: "You never pure loved her, none of you" (p. 218). Darl is unmistakably precise when he describes his father as "a monstrous burlesque of all bereavement" (p. 74).

Addie's dichotomy between saying and doing is somewhat reminiscent of an eschatological saying of Jesus found in Matthew and repeated in Luke with a slight variation. Matthew's version reads: "Not everyone who calls me 'Lord, Lord' will enter the kingdom of Heaven, but only those who do the will of my heavenly Father."[7] Regardless how central to the novel's significance Addie's understanding of the split may appear to be, it is difficult somehow to accept her extreme perspective as the final meaning of the novel. For it is Darl ultimately who sees through both words and deeds to a level of truth that can only be classified by the others as insanity because—and this is Faulkner's revelation to the reader—it is not the way the majority can bear to look at it. Cash would seem to speak with authorial precision when he understands "in a way" (p. 223) why Darl tried to get rid of the body. Although he feels that the destruction of Gillespie's barn was unjustifiable, he cannot avoid the strong realization that Anse has taken the easy way out in having Darl committed. Committing Darl is a denial of "the olden right teaching" (p. 224) that would have us do for others as if we were doing for ourselves. It is because of Darl's acute power of perception—"like he could see through the walls and into the next ten minutes" (p. 226)—that Cash concludes that "this world is not his world; this life his life" (p. 250). Man simply cannot survive the full light of truth, and so he is forced to deflect its brightness.

Within the framework of constitutive apocalyptic symbolism, Faulkner clearly emphasizes the moment of judgment. Addie, whose death is the cause of judgment, determines the canon according to words and deeds. Her insistence on the value of deeds alone is, as we have seen, a variation on an apocalyptic saying of Jesus. Although death is itself a microcosmic image of catastrophe, Faulkner has magnified his treatment of the end through the symbolism of water and fire, traditionally associated with the cosmic cataclysm that brings new life. Jewel is Addie's self-appointed savior; he saves her from water and fire and brings her successfully to her family's burial ground. In the permanence of death, she will be liberated from Anse.

New life is presented in terms of increased awareness and humane concern—and paradoxically in the liberation of confinement; it is not granted simply in accordance with Addie's predilection for deeds. On Addie's scale, Jewel and Cash weighed heavily on the side of deeds; Darl and Anse, on the side of words. The juxtaposition is not the same in view of new life. Jewel who says the least and accomplishes the most—for Addie— recedes into the background once Addie has been interred. The ordeal has revealed his courageous persistence in doing Addie's will, but it has also shown him to be as "private" a person as Addie was. Cash, also a man of deeds, emerges as the one member of the family whose awareness has expanded to perceive the human tensions dividing the family. Of all the Bundrens, Cash alone seems to understand and appreciate, in a way suited to survival, what has happened as a result of Addie's death. He has grown, in Irving Howe's words, "from unimaginative self-containment to humane concern."[8] Death has not merely displaced another human being, as Peabody thinks; it has produced the new life, however modest, of Cash's deepened sensitivity. His awareness of the terrifyingly slow process of human growth to maturity becomes a major perspective of the novel—a realistic view of the new life that the experience of death yields. Anse remains the same severely limited person; the new Mrs. Bundren will be a slave to his sloth just as the first one had been. Darl, although doing least to support

Addie's revenge, is paradoxically freed from the banality of Bundren life when he is committed to the Jackson asylum. Even though the majority of narrative passages are devoted to his perspective, it is his preternaturally perceptive insight into the truth of the family relationships that raises him above his fellow members and makes him ill-suited to remain with them. In being delivered from the circle of their aloneness, he seems unequivocally to have gained.

II

The judgment of words and deeds is less explicit in *Miss Lonelyhearts* than it is in *As I Lay Dying*; it is nevertheless as central to the meaning of West's novel as it is to Faulkner's. Miss Lonelyhearts (Nathanael West gives his advice columnist no other name), whose obsessive concern is to discover some principle of order in the midst of the chaos of existence that he sees pointedly reflected in the letters written to him, is ultimately revealed deficient in both words and deeds. Shrike, the paper's feature editor who pushes the Miss Lonelyhearts column as a scheme to boost circulation, is a type of the loosed Satan who precedes the final catastrophe. The simple, almost stylized narrative that takes Miss Lonelyhearts through the stages of his quest for an answer to the problem of human suffering unfolds against a background of starkly opposed symbols of chaos and order.

The theme of spiritual quest is clear from the very beginning of the novel. Miss Lonelyhearts is a quarter of an hour away from his deadline, and he is still working on his leader; as usual he finds his words flat, insincere, and meaningless. Later, in trying to explain his problem to Betty, Miss Lonelyhearts constructs a parable perfectly descriptive of his own situation: "A man is hired to give advice to the readers of a newspaper. The job is a circulation stunt and the whole staff considers it a joke. . . . He too considers the job a joke, but after several months at it, the joke begins to escape him. He sees that the majority of the letters are profoundly humble pleas for moral and spiritual advice, that they are inarticulate expressions of genuine suffering."[9] Miss Lonelyhearts realizes the impossibility of "finding the same joke funny thirty times a day for months on end," and so he rereads the letters he received that morning, "searching for some clue to a sincere answer" (p. 1). Shrike has given him a piece of white cardboard with a blasphemous parody of the *Anima Christi* on it. It begins: "Soul of Miss L, glorify me" (p. 1). Miss Lonelyhearts has an intuition that Christ really *is* the answer; but since "Christ was Shrike's particular joke," he feels that he must "stay away from the Christ business" (p. 3) to keep from getting sick.

West articulates Miss Lonelyhearts' problem symbolically as a quest for order in the midst of chaos: "Miss Lonelyhearts found himself developing an almost insane sensitiveness to order. Everything had to form a pattern: the shoes under the bed, the ties in the holder, the pencils on the table. . . . For a little while, he seemed to hold his own but one day he found himself with his back to the wall. On that day all the inanimate things over which he had tried to obtain control took the field against him.

When he touched something, it spilled or rolled to the floor. . . . He fled to the street, but there chaos was multiple. Broken groups of people hurried past, forming neither stars nor squares" (pp. 10–11). On the third day of his first illness, Miss Lonelyhearts has these thoughts: "Man has a tropism for order. Keys in one pocket, change in another. Mandolins are tuned G D A E. The physical world has a tropism for disorder, entropy. Man against nature . . . the battle of the centuries. Keys yearn to mix with change. Mandolins strive to get out of tune. Every order has within it the germ of destruction. All order is doomed, yet the battle is worth while" (pp. 30–31).

Aside from several isolated and unambiguous images of apocalypse, there are key symbols of chaos and order in the novel that are fundamentally apocalyptic in meaning. The symbols of chaos are various aspects of nature, human artifacts, and especially human suffering—everything perhaps except human longing. There are also repeated dreams about and instances of violence that support the symbolism of chaos. The single symbol of order is the rock that Miss Lonelyhearts imagines himself becoming.

After his initial frustration in meeting his deadline, Miss Lonelyhearts goes to Delehanty's speakeasy. The gray sky, rubbed clean as if by an eraser, "held no angels, flaming crosses, olive-bearing doves, wheels within wheels" (p. 5). Later, after leaving Betty in a fit of self-righteous rage, "he felt as though his heart were a bomb, a complicated bomb that would result in a simple explosion, wrecking the world without rocking it" (p. 13). Again in Delehanty's he wears "the smile of an anarchist sitting in the movies with a bomb in his pocket" (p. 14).

Nature, supporting Miss Lonelyhearts' abhorrence of the idea and reality of entropy, never really does what it is supposed to. There are no signs of spring even though it is spring: "The decay that covered the surface of the mottled ground was not the kind in which life generates" (p. 4). Miss Lonelyhearts remembers that the previous year it had taken "all the brutality of July to torture a few green spikes through the exhausted dirt" (p. 5). Human artifacts conspire with nature to frighten and shock. The Mexican War obelisk in the park, although structurally a less than obvious suggestion that Miss Lonelyhearts should experiment with sex as a principle of order, seems on the verge of some crude stone orgasm as its shadow lengthens "in rapid jerks, not as shadows usually lengthen." The obelisk is "red and swollen in the dying sun, as though it were about to spout a load of granite seed" (p. 19). The skyscrapers "menaced the little park from all sides" (p. 27). Not even the countryside is different; it is clearly a reverse Eden. "The heavy, musty smell of old furniture and wood rot" (p. 36) makes Betty and Miss Lonelyhearts cough. The flies bother them, and an accidental noise frightens a deer back into the woods. The night noises are disturbing rather than pleasant for a change; and even with the blankets they are cold. Although spring is well advanced, the country is no different from the city:

"In the deep shade there was nothing but death—rotten leaves, gray and white fungi, and over everything a funereal hush" (p. 38).

The analysis of the symbolism of chaos is incomplete without some understanding of Shrike's function in the novel as a warning sign of impending disaster. The *Random House Dictionary* describes a shrike as a predaceous bird that feeds on insects and smaller birds and kills more than it can eat. It has been pointed out that the name is close in sound to Christ, yet different enough to suggest the reverse even before one sees the full development of Shrike's role. He represents the demise of every human value; he is eager to recreate Miss Lonelyhearts in the image of his own appalling insensitivity and total cynicism. He has simply lost his humanity and thus is a perfect herald of final catastrophe in the tradition of the last loosing of Satan.

Certain descriptive touches contribute specifically to the interpretation of Shrike's portrait as demonic. Shrike, the cosmic joker, has chosen Christ as his "particular joke" (p. 3), as we have already mentioned. On his way to Delehanty's, Miss Lonelyhearts decides not to laugh at himself in his frustration because "Shrike was waiting at the speakeasy to do a much better job" (p. 5). One of Shrike's favorite tricks is "used much by moving-picture comedians—the dead pan" (p. 6). No matter how wildly he gesticulates or how excited his speech is, he tries never to change the expression on his face. He claims that it is suffering that drives him "into the arms of the Miss Farkises of this world" (p. 21). Miss Farkis is apparently one of many mistresses. He suffers because his wife was a virgin when she married him and "has been fighting ever since to remain one" (p. 21). Mary, on the other hand, says that the reason why Shrike allows her to go out with other men is "to save money" (p. 22). He allows other men to wine and dine her, then he reaps the sexual benefits of her mellow mood. It is not absolutely clear who is to be believed; one thing is clear, though, and that is that fidelity has little meaning in Shrike's world.

Shrike is the diabolical con man who tries each day to sell Miss Lonelyhearts on some new principle of order for his life, without of course even a hint of sincerity. Shrike recommends that Miss Lonelyhearts give his readers "something new and hopeful" rather than "the same old stuff," so he offers to dictate: "*Art is a Way Out. . . . Art is One of Life's Richest Offerings*. For those who have not the talent to create, there is appreciation" (p. 4). Later he advises Miss Lonelyhearts to "forget the crucifixion, remember the Renaissance" (p. 5). He is especially venomous in his parody of religion. When Miss Farkis announces that she is interested in the "new thomistic synthesis," Shrike asks her whether she has taken them for "stinking intellectuals" or "fake Europeans" (p. 6). He offers her instead, no doubt for Miss Lonelyhearts' benefit, a perfect synthesis for the machine age— a report on an adding machine used as a prayer wheel. Shrike begins a long diatribe called his "Passion in the Luncheonette, or the Agony of the Soda Fountain," which Miss Lonelyhearts understands rightly to be a seduction speech for the benefit of Miss Farkis. Shrike's visceral parable begins: "I am a great saint. . . . I can walk on my own water" (p. 7). He is also, of course, extremely drunk.

After his first sickness, Miss Lonelyhearts considers "how Shrike had accelerated his sickness by teaching him to handle his one escape, Christ, with a thick glove of words" (p. 33). Again at Delehanty's, after insisting that those who have faith are well, not sick, Shrike turns to Miss Lonelyhearts and says, "Come, tell us, brother, how it was that you first came to believe. Was it music in a church, or the death of a loved one, or, mayhap, some wise old priest?" Then, admitting how stupid it was of him not to realize that it was the letters, he proclaims that "the Miss Lonelyhearts are the priests of twentieth-century America" (p. 44). When Shrike reads Peter Doyle's letter containing Fay's accusation of attempted rape, Shrike tells the assembled friends, "This is only one more attempt against him by the devil. He has spent his life struggling with the arch fiend for our sakes, and he shall triumph. I mean Miss Lonelyhearts, not the devil" (p. 54). The gospel according to Shrike that follows, celebrating the long-suffering Miss Lonelyhearts, is nothing but unrelieved cynicism.

The diabolical tone of Shrike's portrayal becomes unmistakably clear when we consider the pattern of his seduction of Miss Lonelyhearts. It is the tripartite structure of the temptation of Jesus found in Matthew and Luke. Here, of course, is the special irony of West's small but vicious apocalypse. Miss Lonelyhearts is Jesus in the wilderness, weaving illusory order out of the chaos of Shrike's temptations, wanting desperately to resist but finally succumbing to Shrike's joke. Miss Lonelyhearts yields to the Pelagian temptation; he comes to believe that *he actually can do it*—bring order out of chaos himself.

Matthew and Luke are apparently both following the same tradition when they amplify Mark's less specific but more primitive account and thus describe Jesus' trial in the wilderness in terms of three (symbolically inclusive) temptations. Although the three temptations are the same in both Gospels, Luke's order (Lk. 4:1–13) inverts the second and third temptations of Matthew (Mt. 4:1–11). It is Luke's order that becomes the structural basis for Shrike's temptation. In Luke there is first of all the temptation to turn stones into bread, then the offer of all the kingdoms of the world if Jesus will do homage to Satan, and finally the temptation to presumption by casting himself from the pinnacle of the temple and expecting the support of God's angels.

Shrike's first temptation is a simple parody of Luke. He encourages Miss Lonelyhearts to give his readers stones rather than bread: "When they ask for bread don't give them crackers as does the Church, and don't, like the State, tell them to eat cake. Explain that man cannot live by bread alone and give them stones. Teach them to pray each morning: 'Give us this day our daily stone'" (p. 5). The second temptation, Shrike's showing Miss Lonelyhearts the universal display of potential principles of order, is spread throughout the narrative. Yet as an ironic moment in Miss Lonelyhearts' ordeal in the wilderness, the panorama of possibilities is summarized in an episode that follows Miss Lonelyhearts' first illness. He has just articulated for himself the tension between chaos and order and the ascendancy of chaos. Shrike recommends the perennial answers to the destructive tendencies of nature. Viewed as potential principles of order, the answers are all escapes from reality. In presenting all the possibilities, Shrike is not above the cynical expression of preference; and thus he mentions in succession and rejects the soil, the South Seas, hedonism, art, suicide, and drugs. He finally reveals his trump card and equivalently asks Miss Lonelyhearts to adore his own special joke: "We are not men who swallow camels only to strain at stools. God alone is our escape. The church is our only hope, the First Church of Christ Dentist, where He is worshipped as Preventer of Decay. The Church whose symbol is the trinity new-style: Father, Son and Wirehaired Fox Terrier" (p. 35).

Shrike's temptations all coalesce in the third; the last temptation is the one that makes the acceptance of Shrike's offer possible because it is the temptation to believe that it really is possible to play God, of one's own accord to bring salvation to the multitudes, to save them through the order in one's own life. At the final party in his apartment, Shrike proposes that they play the game "Everyman his own Miss Lonelyhearts" (p. 51). Each person in the room is to answer one of the letters sent to Miss Lonelyhearts; and from the answer given, Miss Lonelyhearts will diagnose the person's moral ills. "Afterwards," Shrike promises, "he will lead you in the way of attainment" (p. 52). Although it may seem that the malicious Shrike is simply setting the stage to read Peter Doyle's letter exposing Miss Lonelyhearts, the game announces the consummation of a process of temptation that has already taken place. Although he wanted to remain immune to the "Christ business," Miss Lonelyhearts is actually about to succumb to the ultimate degree of presumption when he reaches out to cure Peter Doyle as a confirmation of his identification of himself with God.

Miss Lonelyhearts' gradual fall into presumption is sketched in the developing symbolism of the rock. Throughout, Miss Lonelyhearts has been torn between the natural excitement that he experiences in shouting the name of Christ (and had since his youth in his father's church) and the perplexing fear that acceptance of the Christ answer would put him at Shrike's mercy. He gradually comes to realize that it is not Shrike who prevents him from embracing Christ, but his own lack of humility: "Men have always fought their misery with dreams. . . . He was capable of dreaming the Christ dream. He felt that he had failed at it, not so much because of Shrike's jokes or his own self-doubt, but because of his lack of humility." He vows, therefore, "to make a sincere attempt to be humble" (p. 39), and the outward sign of his essay at humility is his sanctimonious smile. He learns to smile at Shrike "as the saints are supposed to have smiled at those about to martyr them" (p. 44). Accepting Peter Doyle's invitation to dinner, he is "busy with his smile" (p. 45). When Fay Doyle makes a pass at him under the table, Miss Lonelyhearts "paid no attention to her and only broke his beatific smile to drink" (p. 48). Miss Lonelyhearts takes Peter's hand and continues "smiling and holding hands" until Fay calls them "a sweet pair of fairies" (p. 49).

The feigned humility and vapid smile effect Miss
Lonelyhearts' increasing tendency to think of himself as
a rock—solid, unperturbable, immune to the ravages of
chaotic human existence, especially to Shrike. The feature editor bursts into Miss Lonelyhearts' apartment to
invite him to his party; he is a single wave against a rock.
"Shrike dashed against him, but fell back, as a wave that
dashes against an ancient rock, smooth with experience,
falls back. There was no second wave" (p. 51). Dunning
Miss Lonelyhearts to join the party, Shrike becomes "a
gull trying to lay an egg in the smooth flank of a rock, a
screaming, clumsy gull" (p. 51). Mary Shrike sits on
Miss Lonelyhearts' lap in the cab, "but despite her
drunken wriggling the rock remained perfect" (p. 52).
Miss Lonelyhearts withstands the ceaseless waves of
Shrike's rhetoric: "What goes on in the sea is of no
interest to the rock" (p. 53). The sea is a classic symbol
of chaos, and here as throughout this passage the juxtaposition of the primitive symbols is patently apocalyptic.

Betty too could "see the rock he had become" (p. 53).
His mind is touched curiously enough by the realization
that Betty must dress up for special occasions; the rock,
however, remains perfect. His *mind* is "the instrument
with which he knew the rock" (p. 54). While they are
planning for the future, Betty stops laughing and
abruptly begins to cry: "He felt for the rock. It was
still there; neither laughter nor tears could affect the
rock. It was oblivious to wind or rain" (p. 55). The rock,
tested and found perfect, is the "solidification of his
feeling, his conscience, his sense of reality, his self-knowl-
edge" (p. 56). When at the end his fever returns, the

rock is no longer just a part of him; he *is* the rock. "The rock became a furnace" (p. 56).

Miss Lonelyhearts, like the reader, is perfectly prepared for the catastrophe that he creates. He has become the rock, and the rock is God—the foundation of all order, the eternally unchanged in the midst of the changing and changeable. He longs for a sign that will confirm his union with God. And so he decides to attempt a cure of Peter Doyle to prove to himself that "God approve[s] his every thought." The plan is to "embrace the cripple and the cripple would be made whole again, even as he, a spiritual cripple, had been made whole" (p. 57). Doyle comes to Miss Lonelyhearts' apartment, apparently with the intention of killing him for taking liberties with his wife. Miss Lonelyhearts rushes to enclose him in his saving embrace, but Doyle panics. The gun accidentally explodes, and Miss Lonelyhearts dies pathetically in the arms of the cripple he intended to cure.

He is judged for yielding to the ultimate temptation of making himself God; death is his ironic reward for succumbing, against his intentions, to Shrike's joke. Just as the words of his column were empty and meaningless, so were his deeds. He had presumed to do what no man can possibly do.

In *Miss Lonelyhearts*, the symbolism of catastrophe is developed regarding not only the warning signs of disaster, but also the end itself. The tone of impending disaster is established through the classical symbolism of threatening chaos. For Miss Lonelyhearts everything in life is chaotic save man's insatiable longing for order. The symbolism of chaos is composed of the concrete images of unseasonal nature, uncontrollable artifacts, and rampant human misery. Specifically, Shrike's role as tempter is a secular variation of the theme of the loosed Satan; this sign of impending disaster is a thinly disguised traditional symbol. Death is West's apocalyptic symbol of the end; it is the end not only for Miss Lonely-hearts but also, predictably, for all self-appointed saviors of men.

The rock is the primary symbol of order in the novel. Yet we would expect the symbol of order to be an indica-tion of new life; in *Miss Lonelyhearts*, however, it is ironically the revelation of judgment. The rock is the sign of Miss Lonelyhearts' presumption; it is a traditional image for the unchanging fidelity of God. West's imagination projects no future for Miss Lonelyhearts; he is the necessary victim of life's inevitable temptation to put an end to human misery. There is apparently no answer to the problem of evil—certainly not in presump-tion; there is only the frustration of irrepressible desire.

III

A close reading of *As I Lay Dying* and *Miss Lonelyhearts* in relationship to *The Violent Bear It Away* indicates clearly how much Flannery O'Connor was influenced, at least subconsciously, by her attachment to those two novels. Fire and water as symbols of apocalypse play an important part in *The Violent Bear It Away* as they did in *As I Lay Dying*. Both Tarwater and Miss Lonelyhearts try presumptuously to force their own order on creation; the results, however, are strikingly different. There is a curious similarity of emphasis on the tension between words and deeds in all three novels. Yet *The Violent Bear It Away* is by no means a derivative novel. It is unique, even excellent in its own right; and certainly the intensity of its apocalyptic vision is unambiguous.

A general apocalyptic tone is sustained throughout the novel by much of the descriptive imagery associated initially with the latter-day prophet Mason and eventually with Tarwater himself, but not with them exclusively. It is language purposefully imitative of the prophetic and apocalyptic literature of the Bible. As a youth Mason had been called to the city "to proclaim the destruction awaiting a world that had abandoned its Saviour."[10] His message "from the midst of his fury [was] that the world would see the sun burst in blood and fire" (p. 306). Tarwater was satisfied that his great-uncle had really communicated with his God when Mason looked "as if his head were still full of the visions he had seen in its eyes, wheels of light and strange beasts with giant wings of fire and four heads turned to the four points of the universe" (pp. 307–8). When Tarwater has created his own little apocalypse by setting fire to their shack and Mason's body—so he thinks—with it, he imagines he sees the moon bursting through the roof of the shack. As he runs away, he can hear the fire "moving up through the black night like a whirling chariot" (p. 332). When he arrives at Rayber's house and is confronted by Bishop, the revelation comes to him "silent, implacable, direct as a bullet. He did not look into the eyes of any fiery beast or see a burning bush. He only knew, with a certainty sunk in despair, that he was expected to baptize the child he saw." His eyes reflect his own horrifying image of himself "trudging into the distance in the bleeding stinking mad shadow of Jesus, until at last he received his reward, a broken fish, a multiplied loaf" (p. 357).

Rayber, as he awaits the bellow announcing Bishop's baptism-drowning, reflects on his own sense of expectation: "He had had this sense of waiting, kin in degree but not in kind, when he was a child and expected any moment that the city would blossom into an eternal Powderhead. Now he sensed that he waited for a cataclysm. He waited for all the world to be turned into a burnt spot between two chimneys" (p. 421). Tarwater relives the moment of Bishop's passage into eternity; he feels again the child's arms touching him once or twice as he struggles "to extricate himself from a monstrous enclosing darkness" (p. 432).

This general descriptive imagery, though contributing to the pervasive mood of apocalypse, is superficial in comparison with the symbolism of judgment, the substance of Flannery O'Connor's eschatology. Judgment is worked out finally through a pattern of contrasted words and deeds, supported by certain specific and recurring symbols related to hunger, purification, and time. Revelation occurs in the interaction of the principal characters—Mason, Rayber, and Tarwater. Their complex interrelationship is best approached through an analysis of Mason's and Rayber's struggle for the control of Tarwater's education.

Tarwater is torn between two diametrically opposed responses to existence. Although it is clear that he would like to maintain his distance from the philosophies of both Mason and Rayber—respect for mystery and self-reliance—he is nonetheless initially presented a clear-cut choice. In the face of mystery, one *waits* for the revelation of God. Mason had not actually always been able to remember this, however; in his zeal he had been repeatedly inclined to force the hand of God. After he had pronounced judgment upon the sin of the city, destruction had not come. The sun "rose and set and he despaired of the Lord's listening" (p. 306). The Lord finally chastises him for his presumption: "Then one morning he saw to his joy a finger of fire coming out of [the sky] and before he could turn, before he could shout, the finger had touched him and the destruction he had been waiting for had fallen in his own brain and his own body. His blood had been burned dry and not the blood of the world. . . . That was not the last time the Lord had corrected the old man with fire" (p. 306). It was because he had been chastised again and again that Mason felt "he was in a position to instruct Tarwater" (p. 306).

Rayber, Tarwater's schoolteacher uncle, so typical of Flannery O'Connor's intellectuals, is a pitiful creature, almost all mind and no heart. His lack of heart is symbolized by the hearing aid that he wears. The wire going to his head comes out of a metal box on his chest, a heart substitute incapable of running his head. Tarwater is curious to know whether he thinks in the box or in his head; the truth is, for O'Connor, that he does not think at all.

Rayber believes that he has made himself what he is

despite the numerous and almost fatal injections of Mason's Christian nonsense. If he talked about his life being ruined, it was only to impress Mason with the obstacles he had had to overcome in rejecting the old man's poison. Mason had kidnapped Rayber and baptized him at Powderhead when Rayber was only seven. Later, with the wisdom of a liberated twenty-four year old, Rayber is able to tell Mason: "You pushed me out of the real world and I stayed out of it until I didn't know which was which. You infected me with your idiot hopes, your foolish violence. . . . I've straightened the tangle you made. Straightened it by pure will power. I've made myself straight" (p. 346). When Rayber acquires custody of Tarwater, he brags to the snooping Mason, eager to baptize the child: "This one is going to be brought up to live in the real world. He's going to be brought up to expect exactly what he can do for himself. He's going to be his own saviour. He's going to be free!" (p. 345). Despite Rayber's heroic attempts to reeducate Tarwater, the latter continues to show signs of an excessive preoccupation with baptism. Rayber tells him: "The great dignity of man . . . is his ability to say: I am born once and no more. What I can see and do for myself and my fellowman in this life is all of my portion and I'm content with it. It's enough to be a man" (p. 405).

It is clear from the beginning of Tarwater's struggle that he wants to establish his own unique response to life. He definitely intends to stay out of the schoolteacher's head (Mason had unwittingly become the subject of one of Rayber's agnostic magazine articles), and he would also quite clearly like to dislodge Mason's seed from the soil of his brain. When he articulates his plans, it is in terms of a happy medium between waiting and doing, between Mason and Rayber. He tells Meeks, "I mean to wait and see what happens"; and if nothing happens as Meeks supposes, Tarwater concludes: "Then I'll make it happen. . . . I can act" (p. 351). Later he repeats the same idea for Rayber, this time bragging about his imagined victory over Mason in burning the shack. He will wait and see what happens, and if nothing does he will make it happen as he did before (pp. 368–69).

In deciding just what he must do to preserve his individuality, Tarwater rightly senses that his chief adversary is his great-uncle; he is especially plagued by the memory of Mason's mandate to baptize Rayber's idiot child. Rayber poses no real threat to Tarwater; he is as pitiful as the box that lights up his head. The heart of Mason's madness—the hunger for Jesus, the bread of life—is something altogether different. "What he was secretly afraid of was that it might be passed down, might be hidden in the blood and might strike some day in him and then he would be torn by hunger like the old man, the bottom split out of his stomach so that nothing would heal or fill it but the bread of life" (p. 315).

In Flannery O'Connor the created world is always the instrument for the revelation of mystery; and frequently the grotesque is the occasion of theophany. So, expectedly, Tarwater seeks to avoid what he considers to be the "threatened intimacy of creation" by never letting "his eye rest for an instant longer than was needed to place something" (p. 316). He must at all costs avoid stimulating hunger in himself.

That the idiot child Bishop will become the physical offer of grace, the threat of personal revelation, for Tarwater is obvious as soon as he hears the child's breathing over the phone: "He stood there blankly as if he had received a revelation he could not yet decipher. He seemed to have been stunned by some deep internal blow that had not yet made its way to the surface of his mind" (p. 352). When Tarwater first sees Bishop, as we have noted, he has the vision of himself spending his life in "the bleeding stinking mad shadow of Jesus," so direct and unambiguous is the revelation then. He tries "to shout, 'No!' but it was like trying to shout in his sleep" (p. 358). He reacts violently to the boy's friendly gesture and thereafter tries desperately to avoid looking at him. Rayber is perceptive enough to be aware of Tarwater's aversion for the child. He somewhat indignantly tells Tarwater: "I nurse an idiot that you're afraid to look at. . . . Look him in the eye" (p. 389).

One significant and specific reason why Tarwater refuses to look at Bishop, why creation's intimacy seems so particularly threatening here, is that Bishop resembles Mason. Bishop has "pale silver eyes like the old man's except that they were clear and empty" (p. 322). This disturbs Rayber as well: "Rayber knew that the reason Bishop gave him pause was because the child reminded him of the old man. Bishop looked like the old man grown backwards to the lowest form of innocence, and Rayber observed that the boy [Tarwater] strictly avoided looking him in the eye" (p. 371).

It is certainly a curious irony to consider Mason's seed growing into an idiot child, yet so typical is it of Flannery O'Connor's love of the grotesque as an occasion of grace that at least it is not unexpected irony. In a confrontation at the Cherokee Lodge, Rayber admits to Tarwater the influence that Mason had on him, but with reservations: "It fell in us both alike. The difference is that I know it's in me and I keep it under control. I weed it out but you're too blind to know it's in you" (p. 416). Yet creation threatens Rayber at precisely the same point as Tarwater; he experiences periodic irrational urges to love in the presence of Bishop: "The moments would still come when, rushing from some inexplicable part of himself, he would experience a love for the child so outrageous that he would be left shocked and depressed for days, and trembling for his sanity." He normally considered Bishop "as an x signifying the general hideousness of fate, . . . except at the moments when with little or no warning he would feel himself overwhelmed by the horrifying love" (p. 372). He keeps the mysterious urge from getting control of him in much the same way that Tarwater avoids the threatened intimacy—by strict discipline of the eyes. "He did not look at anything too long, he denied his senses unnecessary satisfactions" (p. 373). Ironically, he feels that he can control the urge to love as long as it is focused on Bishop. However, "if anything happened to the child, he would have to face it in itself. Then the whole world would become his idiot child" (p. 410). His attempt to drown Bishop undoubtedly failed because "he had a moment of complete terror in which he envisioned his life without the child" (p. 389).

Since eyes function as the novel's pointed symbol for openness to revealed judgment, it is not surprising that once Tarwater decides it is time to act, in order to assert his individuality, he challenges the intimacy of creation with a stare. Just before Tarwater tells the suspicious lodgekeeper, "You just can't say NO, . . . you got to do NO" (p. 397), she notices that he seems "to see the little boy and nothing else, no air around him, no room, no nothing, as if his gaze had slipped and fallen into the center of the child's eyes and was still falling down and down and down" (p. 396).

In *As I Lay Dying*, words are repudiated altogether, at least by Addie; and in *Miss Lonelyhearts* neither words nor deeds dedicated to bringing order out of chaos seem possible. In *The Violent Bear It Away*, however, effective words and deeds are acknowledged not only as possible, but also as necessarily related—*if* one is responsive to the power of God's judgment. Mason and Tarwater in differing ways manifest this happy marriage of words and deeds. Flannery O'Connor's world is certainly the last one in which the Pelagian hypothesis works; man is simply incapable of saving himself. Rayber, the enlightened modern man for whom science is religion enough, is finally and totally stripped of his self-appointed protection against the mysterious intimacy of creation. Bishop is drowned, and presumably Rayber inherits the idiot world that he feared.

Commenting on Tarwater's baptism-drowning of Bishop in relation to Mason's mandate simply to baptize and Rayber's inability to drown Bishop, Albert Duhamel makes this apparently perceptive remark: "For believers and non-believers alike, [Flannery O'Connor] metamorphoses the act into a metaphoric discriminant between opposed views of history and reality."[11] The observation, however, would seem to have discovered too much and yet too little in the act—too much because it places too sharp a distinction between Mason and Rayber, making them ideological positions rather than unique individuals, and too little because it fails to see the baptism-drowning in the broader context of the novel's judgment of words *and* deeds.

The first person to be presented as failing to back up his words with deeds, or at least as saying too much, is Mason himself. This is, in fact, the first brilliant sketch that we are given of his character. He is a man so wrapped in zeal that he promises more than he can deliver and is himself, therefore, the only one to be chastised after his first prophecy of destruction. It is made quite clear early in the novel that Mason learned his lesson but not in such a way that he was prevented from future mistakes. Mason's rendition of history, especially of family history, seems designed to impress Tarwater; it is more "sell" than zeal. Even Tarwater, as we have noted, is presented as being able to tell in Mason's eyes the extent to which the old man has really experienced the presence of God. Granville Hicks questioned Flannery O'Connor about her preoccupation as a Catholic with fundamentalist preachers, and she responded: "I'm not interested in the sects as sects; I'm concerned with the religious individual, the backwoods prophet.

Old Tarwater [Mason] is the hero of 'The Violent Bear It Away,' and I'm right behind him 100 per cent."[12] It is important to note, therefore, that even though Mason is the prime analogue of integrated saying and doing, he is an individual and not a system, and his inconsistency is delicately portrayed.

Rayber on the other hand is presented as clearly tending in the opposite direction, of saying and never doing. Mason insists that Rayber's "words were one thing and his actions and the look on his face another" (p. 346). Even though Rayber fails totally in his primary effort, namely to free Tarwater as he had supposedly freed himself, he too is drawn with nuance, if not with the subtlety of Mason's characterization.

It is primarily Tarwater, however, whose distinctive response is drawn in terms of saying and doing. Tarwater makes the rash claim to Rayber: "I ain't like you. All you can do is think what you would have done if you had done it. Not me. I can do it. I can act" (p. 418). He can indeed drown Bishop, which Rayber could not even do, but he cannot do what he really claims to do and that is to say *and* do NO in response to the call that came to him through Mason and remains incarnate in Bishop. He persists in his semi-delusion when nervously repeating his experience for the auto-transit truckdriver: "There are them that can act and them that can't, and them that are hungry and them that ain't. That's all. I can act. And I ain't hungry" (p. 428). Always protesting too much, Tarwater here summarizes his supposed ascendancy over both Rayber and Mason. Yet he has actually spoken the words of baptism even as he was drowning the child, and he cannot manage to assuage his hunger. The reality of the situation is that the mysterious power of God has begun to draw him gratuitously to his mission.

Commentators fret over the question of Tarwater's freedom, asking how in any sense he can be said to have baptized Bishop freely.[13] The reason this scene is so important for them is that they have made it the turning point in Tarwater's acceptance of the prophetic call. They fail to notice that Tarwater continues to run from his destiny even after the baptism-drowning. Actually this mysterious episode functions in the scheme of the novel like the first impulse to faith; in O'Connor's Roman Catholic world, that first impulse is a free gift from God, and not a question of human freedom at all. His own disturbed psyche has vomited out the words of baptism. He may be unsuccessful in repressing the promptings of grace, yet he is not determined to accept his mission. The question of Tarwater's freedom can be adequately answered only in discerning the significance of the homosexual rape. It is the mysterious gesture of grace in the midst of sordid physical exploitation that Tarwater actually responds to freely. Only when he experiences evil personally can he understand the enduring need for preaching "the terrible speed of justice" (p. 339). Moreover, knowledge that Mason has after all been buried by Buford Munson brings with it a confirming grace of realization that his efforts at self-salvation have been frustrated from the beginning. The ultimate judgment is that man is most human when he is open to the rhythm of revelation, when he allows himself to be truly surprised by the intimacy of creation. Our most effectual deeds are those that most genuinely respond to God's word of revelation.

The apocalyptic motif of the novel is emphasized through a number of related symbols: the symbolism of hunger, generally associated with eschatology; the symbolism of fire and water, traditional signs of purifying chaos; and finally the numerical symbolism of completion implicit in the time sequence of the novel. The symbolism of hunger for the bread of everlasting life is so patent and pervasive that it needs no further critical treatment, and the symbolism of water has hopefully been suggested adequately in the commentary on the baptism-drowning. I will concentrate here, therefore, on the apocalyptic symbolism of fire and on the significance of the temporal sequence of the novel.

Tarwater uses fire three times in the course of the novel, once in the beginning and twice at the end, so that the narrative is circumscribed by its purifying presence. He burns the shack in which he believes Mason still to be, hoping thereby to *do* something that will sign his desired denial of the resurrection. Thus Tarwater's first use of fire is an abortive refusal of grace; seven days later he ritualizes his acceptance of inner purification. On the final day of the novel, like the beginning a day of passage, Tarwater burns the ground where his body had been violated by the homosexual and the woods at Powderhead where the sibilant inner voice of the "stranger" makes a final attempt to seduce his soul. The description suggests that the homosexual is simply an incarnation of the diabolical stranger within. Both are portrayed as wearing panama hats (pp. 324, 438); the eyes of the homosexual seem lavender (p. 438), of the stranger violet (p. 431); and a sweet odor is associated with both (pp. 439, 444).

Fire is the apocalyptic instrument of Tarwater's initiation into the new life of prophetic service. Mason hoped that he had trained Tarwater to distinguish between the evils that come from the world and those that "come from the Lord and burn the prophet clean; for he himself had been burned clean and burned clean again. He had learned by fire" (p. 306). Tarwater's purification by fire occurs in his realization of experienced evil at the hands of the homosexual: "His eyes looked small and seedlike as if while he was asleep, they had been liftd out, scorched, and dropped back into his head" (p. 441). The repetition of the image of purification associated with Mason's cleansing is confirmation of the fact that Tarwater's positive response to his call takes place at this point in the narrative—and freely. His eyes reveal the realization that has been burned into his soul. Once purified, he will undertake the mission of cleansing others, as Mason had predicted. On the back of the magazine that had carried Rayber's article about him, Mason had scrawled: "THE PROPHET I RAISE UP OUT OF THIS BOY WILL BURN YOUR EYES CLEAN" (pp. 391–92).

Moreover, there is an apocalyptic pattern implicit in the time sequence of the novel. The narrative covers eight days, a temporal sequence that can be divided reasonably into two periods of meaning: the day of Mason's death and the summation of the period of Tarwater's training, followed by a week in which Tarwater

struggles with the call on his own terms. It is at midnight
of the seventh day of *his* week that Tarwater begins his
new life as prophet. The number seven, as we have noted
before, is an apocalyptic image of completion; it supports our acceptance of the fact that his prophetic initiation is indeed consummated. Although the light of the
new week has not dawned, Tarwater has nonetheless set
his face "toward the dark city, where the children of
God [lie] sleeping" (p. 447).

Finally, the very title Flannery O'Connor has given to
her novel reveals the scope of her apocalyptic imagination. The title page indicates that the words are taken
from Matthew's Gospel, but to begin to understand their
meaning in relation to the novel we must work with the
entire verse. Flannery O'Connor cites the Douay trans-
lation: "From the days of John the Baptist until now,
the kingdom of heaven suffereth violence, and the violent bear it away" (Mt. 11:12). Ronald Knox's transla-
tion, that she could easily have consulted to elucidate the
meaning of the Douay text, renders the verse in this way:
"Ever since John the Baptist's time, the kingdom of
heaven has opened to force; and the forceful are even
now making it their prize." The verse is extremely difficult to translate, and it is no wonder that unanimity of
interpretation is totally lacking.

In translating the latter part of the verse, the confusion has always been whether the men of violence are
enemies of the kingdom or enthusiasts. Stanley Edgar
Hyman, for example, in a hermeneutical exercise that
shows clearly how one ought not to proceed, decides
what the verse means by comparing translations (Au-

thorized Version and New English Bible) and then applies his interpretation to the novel: "Its [the verse's] clear meaning is that the violent are enemies of the kingdom, capturing it from the righteous, as a sign of the imminent coming of the Messiah, the Christ. In this sense the Tarwaters are mad fanatics carrying away the kingdom from its lukewarm heirs, and Rayber is an equally mad fanatic preaching secular salvation."[14] Hyman's interpretation seems erroneous for more reasons than simply his inversion of the hermeneutical process.

The only reasonable way to proceed would seem to be from the novel and the author's world to the sense that she probably attributed to the text from Matthew. Carter Martin in his recent critical study, although reading properly from book to title, succumbs nevertheless to the defect of simple excess in interpreting the title. He sees both Tarwater and Rayber, believer and nonbeliever, as indicated by the title, one supporting the kingdom by violence, the other potentially destroying it.[15] But violence implies the capacity to act, and in O'Connor's world Rayber is clearly impotent. Considering the manner in which the kingdom has manifested itself to Tarwater—in the sacramental presence of an idiot child whose baptism is a violent drowning and, especially, through rape by a homosexual—it seems safe to say that an understanding of Jesus' saying about violence and the kingdom that obviously appealed to Flannery O'Connor is that in moments of special revelation (as the days between John the Baptist and Jesus undoubtedly were) the grace of God seizes men violently.

Moreover, it is incontestable that O'Connor understood violence as a mark of the enthusiast. In an interview with Sister Mariella Gable, she spoke of fanaticism as a sign of intensity of belief:

> To a lot of Protestants I know, monks and nuns are fanatics, none greater. And to a lot of monks and nuns I know, my Protestant prophets are fanatics. For my part, I think the only difference between them is that if you are a Catholic and have this intensity of belief you join the convent and are heard no more; whereas if you are a Protestant and have it, there is no convent for you to join and you go about the world getting into all sorts of trouble and drawing the wrath of people who don't believe anything much at all down on your head.[16]

In commenting on her story "A Good Man is Hard to Find," she said on another occasion: "Violence is never an end in itself. It is the extreme situation that best reveals what we are essentially. . . . Violence is a force which can be used for good or evil, and among other things taken by it is the kingdom of heaven. But regardless of what can be taken by it, the man in the violent situation reveals those qualities least dispensable in his personality, those qualities which are all he will have to take into eternity with him."[17] Frederick Hoffman is most accurate therefore when he sees violence in the novel as "a quality of the religious act."[18] Moreover, he avoids the intentional fallacy, even though he is regrettably timid in applying his perceptive observation to the biblical text.

Thus the interpretation of the verse that seems most in accord with the meaning of the novel and the demands of Flannery O'Connor's fictional world is this: The kingdom of heaven manifests itself violently, and men in violence take hold of it. "Men in violence" refers not only to the effect of the manifestation of the kingdom upon the one called (Tarwater's scorched eyes), but also to his emotionally total response (the zealous night march toward the sleeping city). The author's apocalyptic imagination strives to keep before the reader the extreme situation because it is this situation that best reveals to us what we are essentially; it is also clearly *in* the violent situation that our response is purest, drained of all self-interest and especially of facile optimism, which for her is the true enemy of faith.

From Jeremiah on through the ages of the Judaeo-Christian experience, violence has been a mark of the prophet. Jesus, as the text from Matthew indicates, saw the intensification of conflict to be a sign of his inauguration of the Messianic kingdom announced by John the Baptist. Following his great-uncle Mason, Tarwater is an heir to this tradition: "He felt his hunger [for the kingdom] no longer as a pain but a tide. He felt it rising in himself through time and darkness, rising through the centuries, and he knew that it rose in a line of men whose lives were chosen to sustain it, who would wander in the world, strangers from that violent country where the silence is never broken except to shout the truth" (pp. 446–47).

The Violent Bear It Away is rich in apocalyptic symbolism. Although I have not stressed the apocalyptic significance of the inner stranger, it is clear that in interpreting the homosexual as the incarnation of the stranger I have associated the stranger unmistakably with evil. His persistent efforts to divert Tarwater from his prophetic vocation suggest the activity of Satan in his last brief loosing. Since Tarwater, like Mason, had sought to take things into his own hands, he too is judged for his presumption; one *waits* for the revelation of mystery, Tarwater learns. He is judged both by water and by fire. His drowning of Bishop becomes the child's baptism, against Tarwater's wishes. And after he has been violated by the homosexual, his scorched eyes indicate that he has been burned by the personal experience of evil; the fire of God's permissive grace burns the arrogance from his defiant eyes.

Yet, because fire and water are used consciously as symbols of purification, they clearly represent an end that is a beginning. The water is Bishop's passage into the new life of his true country. The fires that Tarwater sets to cleanse symbolically his ravished body and mind signal his passage into the new life of prophecy. The novel clearly emphasizes the imagery of new life. The motif of hunger for the kingdom of God is perhaps the principal strand of the symbolism of renewal. The object of the hunger is the bread of life, and it is this properly speaking that is the symbol of new life. The hunger itself is the expression in Mason and Tarwater of the incompleteness of their earthly life. The final image of the heavenly hillside and the multiplication of the loaves is eschatological imagery taken directly from the Gospels. The time sequence of eight days, extending beyond the symbolic completion of the week, confirms the expectation of the dawn of new life. As the novel ends, Tarwater emerges from the darkness of his period of prophetic trial into the light of his new life as prophet.

CHAPTER FOUR

Ellison, Baldwin, and Wright:

Vestiges of Christian Apocalypse

The apocalyptic tradition has had a profound influence on the Afro-American imagination. Although I will not be concerned in this chapter with patterns of literary indebtedness, the fact of the specific influence of this tradition upon the best contemporary black writers of fiction can hardly be denied. No doubt, the religious heritage of the black man in America and his understandable impatience in the face of racist oppression have helped to generate the mood of impending disaster that is characteristic of the black imagination in America today. These general questions of religious and social influence are undoubtedly important and deserve close consideration, but they are outside the scope of this chapter.

The outstanding contributions of recent black authors to American literature have been dominated by the mood and images of apocalypse. I have chosen works, therefore, that will illustrate the scope of the contemporary Afro-American imagination. In the order of publication, they are Richard Wright's *Native Son* (1940), Ralph Ellison's *Invisible Man* (1952), and James Baldwin's *Go Tell It on the Mountain* (1953). I will be concerned not so much with the similarities that can be found in these three writers as with the differences in apocalyptic imagery and tone that can be discerned in their novels. The basis for selecting the works is the critical consensus concerning the significant black writers of fiction of the past three decades. In the case of Wright and Baldwin I have chosen the novel that is generally considered to be the author's best; from Ellison, the only one he has written to date.

The events of Christian apocalypse that will be pertinent to my analysis are (1) the last loosing of Satan, (2) the final catastrophe in which the world will be destroyed and history as we know it will come to an end, and (3) the appearance of the new heaven and the new earth. These "events" reduced to cyclic symbolism are characteristic also of primitive religious apocalypse. It is within this framework that my analysis of the nature and causes of catastrophe will be worked out, at least to the extent that a secular analogue of these events will be a key to the apocalyptic vision of the writer.

Baldwin's novel alone, among those under consideration, has a specifically Christian imaginative setting. Thus, in the others, the last loosing of Satan is drawn in terms of images of chaos and confusion, of personal doubt and rampant hypocrisy. Catastrophe is presented in terms of violence and riot, the "historical vengeance" that Baldwin sees Americans inadvertently perpetrating. Judgment is the author's revelation of the specific "sin" of man that has triggered the cataclysm. And the new creation, ironically, becomes the sense of accomplishment and personal dignity that violence alone can achieve. But this is obviously not the renewal of normative apocalypse.

I

The distinctive feature of late Hebrew and early Christian apocalyptic literature was that the final events were envisioned as taking place in the future. The Reformation and Puritan phases of apocalyptic writing saw the various moments of apocalypse as either past or present. It is this phase of our Western tradition that has had the greatest influence on the Afro-American apocalyptic imagination. The present in Ralph Ellison's *Invisible Man* is the very period of the last loosing of Satan.

The secular counterpart of Satan, master of chaos and confusion, is the Reverend Bliss P. Rinehart, "spiritual technologist," pastor of the "Holy Way Station," who invites the public to join him in the "*NEW REVELA-TION* of the *OLD TIME RELIGION*."[1] It is precisely the moment when the narrator of the novel becomes aware of Rinehart's existence that the riot breaks out in Harlem—the riot that was foreshadowed in the beginning of the novel by the "battle royal" in the presence of the leading white citizens of the narrator's home town and by the bedlam at the Golden Day and which becomes a threatening possibility as soon as the narrator steps out of the subway in Harlem and hears Ras the Exhorter haranguing the crowd.

Running from Ras, the Exhorter become Destroyer, the narrator disguises himself with dark glasses and a white hat and is repeatedly mistaken for Rinehart. It is thus he learns the many disguises of the loosed Satan: "Rine the runner and Rine the gambler and Rine the briber and Rine the lover and Rinehart the Reverend" (p. 430). Adding Rine the rounder and Rine the rascal, he asks himself what integrity can conceivably mean in a world in which Rinehart is not only possible, but successful. Rinehart is the protean face of fraud, the incarnation of hypocrisy, the superpromiser who keeps one reaching out toward a future that persistently eludes one's grasp. Ellison himself has commented on his conception of Rinehart, an intention masterfully realized in the novel: "Rinehart is my name for the personification of chaos. He is also intended to represent America and change. He has lived so long with chaos that he knows how to manipulate it. It is the old theme of *The Confidence-Man*. He is a figure in a country with no solid past or stable class lines; therefore he is able to move about easily from one to the other."[2]

Rinehart is not only real, he seems to be reality itself. In each of the the three portions of the narrative, beginning with a piece of paper that sets the nameless hero running (Ellison himself has acknowledged the three-fold framework of the novel),[3] there are three promisers who contribute to the chaotic experience of the narrator—all made in the likeness of and foreshadowing the superpromiser himself, Rinehart.

The first unit of the novel begins with the narrator's acceptance of a scholarship to the state college for Negroes. His grandfather instructs him in a dream to read the document. Its message, he says, is clear: "To Whom It May Concern . . . Keep This Nigger-Boy Running" (p. 35). The central promisers of the first section are the school superintendent, Norton, and Bledsoe. The school superintendent, in the name of the Board of Education, presents the narrator with a briefcase containing the scholarship, but only after the humiliating "battle royal" and the faltering delivery of his graduation speech on humility as the lot of his people. Mr. Norton, the wealthy white trustee of the Negro college, speaks of the success of the college as if he were chiseling his own destiny out of inanimate natural resources, when in reality all he wants is a living memorial to his dead daughter. Dr. Bledsoe, the black president of the college, suspends the narrator from school for letting Mr. Norton meet Jim Trueblood and see the Golden Day, showing that his interest in white-endowed academe is really a thirst for power. Fraudulent self-interest alone could make him say, "I'll have every Negro in the country hanging on tree limbs by morning if it means staying where I am" (p. 128).

Bledsoe promises letters of introduction to New York friends of the school so that the nameless hero can gain some profitable experience during the period of his suspension. The suspension is actually expulsion, and the letters of introduction are only more sophisticated versions of "Keep This Nigger-Boy Running." "I beg you, sir," the letter reads, "to help him [a former student of ours] continue in the direction of that promise which, like the horizon, recedes ever brightly and distantly beyond the hopeful traveler" (p. 168)—or, as the youthful protagonist interprets it, "Hope him to death, and keep him running" (p. 171).

Thus, the second piece of paper opens the middle portion of the narrative in which the black youth meets Mr. Emerson (who reveals the content of the letter of introduction to him), Lucius Brockway, and Brother Jack. Weak victim of his father and a business world he is ill-suited for, Mr. Emerson can promise apparently only a homosexual liaison. "Uncle Tom" Brockway, underground guardian of the Liberty Paint Company, where Optic White is the Right White, would rather kill than let a union member usurp his position of control. Brother Jack, needing a new Booker T. Washington to serve the cause of History and Change, gives the eloquent young narrator a new name and sets him running for the Brotherhood of Man, with the assurance that all he has to do is "work hard and follow instructions" (p. 267). There is no difference obviously between Rinehartism and the Brotherhood; both are based on the "realistic" assumption that it is impossible *not* to take advantage of people—"the trick is to take advantage of them in their own best interest" (p. 436).

The third and climactic portion of the novel begins with the threatening anonymous note, which the black youth later discovers was written by Brother Jack himself; it warns him that "this is a white man's world" (p. 332) and they will cut him down if he goes too fast. The masters of chaos of this final strand are Ras the Exhorter-become-Destroyer, Sybil, and Rinehart himself, all of whom keep the narrator running—literally. Ras, a militant black nationalist, drives the protagonist into the anonymous world of dark glasses and white hat, convinced that his association with the white-dominated Brotherhood is hurting the black cause. The riot breaks out shortly after Ras announces that "the *time has come*" (p. 419). "A new Ras of a haughty, vulgar dignity," obviously not above a little personal glory, rides on a great black horse through the streets of Harlem during the riot that he has wanted so badly, "dressed in the costume of an Abyssinian chieftain" (p. 481). The narrator, hoping that he can find out what the Brotherhood actually thinks of him, goes to Sybil, wife of one of the Brothers and a comic imitation of the Cumaean sibyl consulted by Aeneas before his descent into Hades. She knows nothing though; she is simply the paradigm of the white liberal wives who confuse "the class struggle with the ass struggle" (p. 362). Unable almost to elude her, the "hero" runs pell-mell from the pursuing Sybil into the jaws of rioting Harlem, where the sights and sounds are suggestive of the very atmosphere of hell. A little later in mad flight from the Destroyer, he goes underground literally when he stumbles into an open manhole and decides to remain there so that he can "think things out in peace, or, if not in peace, in quiet" (p. 494).

This summary of the three segments of the novel,

which unfortunately may have made a complex work of art seem somewhat artificial, has, I hope, demonstrated the fact that in Ellison's secular apocalypse Rinehart is not the only satan, but rather the last and greatest of a long line of artful deceivers and hypocritical promisers; for in the world of *Invisible Man*, their name is legion. It is no doubt significant that Rinehart himself never appears in the novel; yet he seems to be known by everyone but the narrator. Chaos is simply the characteristic feature of life.

Despite the prevalence of apocalyptic imagery which intensifies the atmosphere of mounting racial conflict and culminates in the riot of the oppressed people of Harlem, Ellison has not written a protest novel. He has instead used the images of catastrophe as a medium for writing a brilliant parable about modern man's quest for identity in which man is no longer either *faber* or *sapiens*, but homo *invisibilis*.

The narrator comes to a realization of his invisibility as he stumbles through a world of chaos of which Rinehart is the living symbol. With so many people around anxious to use him for their own ends, he begins to wonder whether he is "a man or a natural resource" (p. 263). The acceptance of a world in which Rinehart is not only real but viable throws light on his experience of the long line of promisers, and he realizes that all of them had kept him from himself by attempting to force their own picture of reality on him. "If only we had some true friends," he reflects, "some who saw us as more than convenient fools for shaping their own de-

sires" (p. 441). He has had to become invisible before
he realizes that he is nobody but himself.

Exhausted by running for and from the Brotherhood,
he had taken momentary solace in doing what he could
to hasten the catastrophe. His dying grandfather's message to the family had been "to overcome 'em with yeses,
undermine 'em with grins, agree 'em to death and destruction" (pp. 19–20). And the vet at the Golden Day
had advised him, "Play the game, but don't believe in it"
(p. 137). Then the solution must be that if he could
not help the Brotherhood to see reality, he could at least
help them "to ignore it until it exploded in their faces"
(p. 442).

Yet when the riot begins and he sees "the absurdity of
the whole night"—the puddles of oil and milk in the
street (ironic parody of the "milk and honey" of the
promised land), the seven mannequins hanging before
the gutted store, and Ras on a horse, he realizes that he
no longer has "to run for or from the Jacks and the
Emersons and the Bledsoes and Nortons, but only from
their confusion, impatience, and refusal to recognize the
beautiful absurdity of their American identity" (p. 483)
and his. And he realizes too that it is "better to live out
one's own absurdity than to die for that of others,
whether for Ras's or Jack's" (p. 484). For the truth of
the matter is that they were not the only ones to blame.
Even though they had made him invisible, he had coop-
erated because he had refused to accept the risk of his
own humanity. "The fact is that you carry part of your
sickness within you," he admits, " . . . there *is* a death in

the smell of spring and in the smell of thee as in the smell
of me" (pp. 497, 502). In a final encounter with Mr.
Norton, he shares his insight with his old benefactor:
"Take any train; they all go to the Golden D—"
(p. 500).

The real problem had lain in thinking that Rinehart
and invisibility were the only possibilities. No, he reflects
finally, "Life is to be lived, not controlled; and humanity
is won by continuing to play in face of certain defeat"
(p. 499).

Somehow, the day of wrath has given birth, if not to
a new earth, at least to a new atom of love—but not
phony forgiveness, he assures us, because he is indeed a
"desperate man" (p. 501). Words have always been his
forte; it was his oratorical skill that gained him his position with the Brotherhood. Thus, in sharing his experience of chaos, he has shown himself through art to be
in some sense the master of chaos. He has given form and
meaning to his experience by sharing his story with
others. "In order to get some of it down I *have* to love"
(p. 501), he concludes. As R. W. B. Lewis has suggested,
Invisible Man is indeed the narrative equivalent of the
blues, bearing the same significance that Ellison himself
has attributed to the musical form: "The blues is an
impulse to keep the painful details and episodes of a brutal experience alive in one's aching consciousness, to
finger its jagged grain, and to transcend it, not by the
consolation of philosophy but by squeezing from it a
near-tragic, near-comic lyricism. . . . [It is the] chronicle
of personal catastrophe expressed lyrically."[4]

In *Invisible Man* there is almost exclusive emphasis on

the symbolism of the warning signs of catastrophe. The threefold structure of the novel exposes the varieties of deception that permeate the life of modern man. One after the other, the masks of exploitation are lifted; the myriad impersonal ways in which we are rendered invisible by modern society are judged. The con man Rinehart, the last of a long line of deceivers, is the personal embodiment of the evil that has been lurking deceptively in the shadows of the narrator's life. Rinehart is the secular analogue of the loosed Satan. Once his presence is known, it is already too late to avert the riot. The threefold structural rhythm of the warning signs of disaster intensifies the tone of urgency that Ellison seems bent on imparting. The riot, a symbol of secular catastrophe, pales in significance when compared with the emphasis on the peril of the loosed Satan.

Despite the suggestion that once Rinehart is recognized for what he is it is already too late to avert the riot, there is the positive note of the narrator's realization that he has actually allowed himself to be exploited and so deserves blame too. Ellison seems to be aware of the possibility, however paradoxical, of a spark of love illuminating the mass of invisible faces. Moreover, in the very act of telling the story of modern man, one alleviates some of the suffering by imposing artistic order upon the chaos of experience.

II

James Baldwin's expressed intention as a writer of fiction is to dissolve the stereotype of the Negro "as a social phantom of hatred-and-condescension"[5] and to provide instead a variety of personalities, in all of their individuality and complexity. Yet despite the fact that he repudiates the "protest novel," he may well, as Steven Marcus has observed, have written the most powerful one of all.[6] Such is the artistic effect in *Go Tell It on the Mountain* of his efforts "to tell it the way it is."

The novel begins on "the seventh day," the last day of the week and suggestive as well of the last age of the world, and ends on the morning of the eighth—the first day of the new creation, the day of ultimate salvation. It is the fourteenth birthday of John Grimes and the day of his first (and possibly last) experience of salvation. There are two opposing symbols in the novel, the city and the church. The city is the city of perdition, the city of the white man, viewed by John first from a hill in Central Park and then at closer quarters on a brief but tempting excursion through its streets. The city is indeed real and alluring, but John has been told and realizes that it is inaccessible to him. The church of his people, which promises "unimaginable" glory, is indeed his and their only possession—the mountain of holiness, the only one that he can and must climb. Their faith is based on a literal acceptance of God's word; its atmosphere is one of impending doom, of the fateful and imminent visitation of God's wrath upon sinners.

John awakens on the morning of his birthday with a frightening sense of "menace in the air around him."[7] The apocalyptic atmosphere of his family's faith has conditioned the interpretation of his feelings: "He could believe, almost, that he had awakened late on that great

getting-up morning; that all the saved had been transformed in the twinkling of an eye, and had risen to meet
Jesus in the clouds, and that he was left, with his sinful
body, to be bound in hell a thousand years" (p. 18). He
is aware that he has sinned; yet the real darkness of his
sin is in his refusal to accept God's power because he does
not want to be like his father—a self-righteous preacher
of God's word who keeps the atmosphere of their home
charged with his proud warnings of impending wrath
because he must overcompensate emotionally for "the
lions of lust and longing that [once] prowled the de-
fenseless city of his mind" (p. 94). John fears that he
cannot "bow before the throne of grace without first
kneeling to his father" (p. 21), and this he will never do.

It is Saturday and his father is expected home early.
Faced with the prospect of an afternoon of prayer led
by his father, John allows himself a brief excursion into
the "city of perdition." With the money his mother has
given him for his birthday he decides to see a movie;
and in the darkness of the theater, his mood is apprehen-
sively apocalyptic: "He waited for this darkness to be
shattered by the light of the second coming, for the ceil-
ing to crack upward, revealing, for every eye to see, the
chariots of fire on which descended a wrathful God and
all the host of Heaven" (p. 38). Even the movie is no
relief because he imagines that God has allowed him to
see it in order "to show him an example of the wages of
sin" (p. 40). When he reaches home, the atmosphere is
charged with fresh tension; his brother Roy has received
a knife wound in a fight with a white gang and his father

is raving about "what white folks does to niggers" (p. 46).

Thus begins the long ordeal of the night of prayer at the Temple of the Fire Baptized. With masterful technique, Baldwin weaves the fabric of the family's history as Florence, Gabriel, and Elizabeth pray in the midst of the "saints." They are personal histories of fleeting love, of consuming passion, of enduring hatred, but also social histories of the tragic limitation of possibilities, of people nominally free yet imprisoned behind barriers infinitely more oppressive than bars. And herein lies the power of Baldwin's unintended protest, the simple yet dramatic evocation of shared experiences that cry out for vengeance.

The culmination of the evening of prayer is John's experience of salvation, prompted no doubt by his adolescent admiration and affection for Elisha, a slightly older boy who has already tasted the sweetness of God's mercy and who now teaches at the Temple. After the prolonged emotional agony of his religious experience, John desires to speak the "living word" that could heal the division between himself and his father; but it will not come. He at least announces his salvation and repeats a text that he has heard his father use.

The effect of his religious experience is expressed in the apocalyptic imagery of the beauty and bliss of the heavenly city. As John and Elisha walk back through the streets of Harlem toward home and rest, John's inner peace is reflected in the surroundings. "And the avenue, like any landscape that has endured a storm, lay changed under Heaven, exhausted and clean, and new. Not again, forever, could it return to the avenue it once had been. Fire, or lightning, or the latter rain, coming down from these skies which moved with such pale secrecy above him now, had laid yesterday's avenue waste, had changed it in a moment, in the twinkling of an eye, as all would be changed on the last day, when the skies would open up once more to gather up the saints" (pp. 215–16).

A confirmation of the mood of the new creation that John experiences is implicit in the narrative technique that Baldwin uses to unify the final scene. The saints have been returning from the Temple in three groups, and we are permitted successively to get their reactions to the night of prayer and healing. An ambulance siren—"the headlong, warning bell" (p. 211)— pierces the early morning quiet; it is clearly a secular image of impending catastrophe. We hear the siren three times, from the perspective of each of the three walking groups. "Another soul struck down" and "He said in the last days evil would abound" (p. 209) are the reactions of Sister McCandless and Sister Price. Florence comments to Gabriel, "That wagon's coming, ain't it, one day for everybody?" (p. 211). But the third group, John and Elisha, indicates no reaction at all. The inference is clear; because the Lord's day has already dawned for John, he is beyond experience of this sign of doom, momentarily absorbed in the joy of salvation.

I say "momentarily" because there is no reason to assume—by analogy with the others in the novel who have had similar experiences—that the joy of the new creation will, in any sense, be permanent. Moreover, when John senses the transformation of the Harlem street, the author notes ironically that it will reveal its actual horror to him again shortly. The transitory character of the experience of salvation simply heightens the tragedy of these people for whom religion is a solitary possession. Steven Marcus has accurately delineated the place of religion in their lives: "Religion offers coherence to otherwise chaotic lives and permits them to go on living without destroying themselves. It does not cure their ailments, or stop their sinning, or change their personalities."[8] They are isolated from their fellow men, and yet far from God —like their fellow men. Gabriel's prayer during the tarry service expresses the tragedy more poignantly: "They were dishonored, their very names were nothing more than dust blown disdainfully across the field of time— to fall where, to blossom where, bringing forth what fruit hereafter, where?—their very names were not their own. Behind them was the darkness, nothing but the darkness, and all around them destruction, and before them nothing but the fire—a bastard people, far from God, singing and crying in the wilderness!" (p. 137).

If *Invisible Man* concentrates on the secular analogue of the last loosing of Satan, *Go Tell It on the Moutain* emphasizes the illusory nature of the experience of new life after the ordeal of faith. Baldwin relies upon the Christian imagery of the expectation of the Second Coming. If judgment of personal sin is uppermost in the mind of John Grimes before his experience of faith, the novel itself judges the effect of faith to be illusory at best. John stands in personal need of the liberating religious experience of the Temple of the Fire Baptized; as an adolescent, he is perhaps even more in need of the love of his idol Elisha, his guide in the way of faith. Yet the real judgment of the novel is not of John's adolescent sins but of white Christianity that has used faith in the crucified Jesus as a way of keeping the black man content with his lot. The image of the heavenly city, already come to earth in the morning streets of Harlem, is the ultimate of ironies. The belief in the new life of eternity —for the black man in America, at least—is self-defeating. There is no new life in continued oppression. The faith that teaches humble acceptance of one's earthly lot in view of an eternal reward must, in fact, be rejected if there is to be any life at all.

III

Unlike *Go Tell It on the Mountain*, which speaks realistically of shared experiences, Richard Wright's *Native Son* is professedly and unambiguously a novel of protest. Certainly the tone of this novel is more starkly apocalyptic than the others because, in presenting the oppression of a people in terms of the fate of one man, *Native Son* is unrelieved by even the hint of humor. Wright's moment of apocalypse is not the last loosing of Satan even though one can readily see the family resemblance of Mr. and Mrs. Dalton, Britten, and Buckley to Norton, Bledsoe, and the Brotherhood. Mr. and Mrs. Dalton have Norton's sense of destiny in assuming the "white man's burden" of educating Negroes. Britten, who conducts his first investigation of Bigger in the red glare of a furnace, is like some cruel judge of the underworld who assumes guilt regardless of the facts. And Buckley, whose "white face" glares at Bigger from a newly pasted political poster as the novel begins, is the archetypal manipulator of public fear and hatred to his personal advantage.

As prominent as these personalities are, they are a key to the dominant imagery of the novel only insofar as they fuse together and become part of the all-encompassing cold white world. In stark opposition to the images of whiteness and coldness are those related to the tension and passion that build to the breaking point within Bigger. When analyzing these opposing strands of imagery, one is curiously reminded of "Fire and Ice," Robert Frost's somewhat whimsical venture into eschatology. Because of his experience of desire, the poet insists that he must side with those who claim the world will end by fire; nevertheless, he knows the power of hatred well enough to say that "for destruction ice/ Is also great/ And would suffice."[9] Richard Wright's answer in *Native Son* seems unequivocally to be fire *and* ice, or fire *because of* ice. In order to understand the act of violence which is Bigger's response to oppression, some attention must be given to the juxtaposition of these strands of imagery.

The world which releases the violence pent up in Bigger is cold, white, and blind. The first sight to greet Bigger when he emerges from his tenement on Chicago's South Side is Buckley's white face on the signboard poster.[10] Bigger and his friends watch a skywriter leave "a slender streak of billowing white blooming against the deep blue," that becomes "a long trail of white plumage" (p. 19). The presence of the plane and its white plumage is significant because Bigger's great desire had been to be a pilot—an impossible dream in his white-dominated world. The friends play a game called "white" in which they live in fantasy in "the vast white world that sprawled and towered in the sun before them" (p. 21). The white neighborhood where the Daltons live is "a cold and distant world; a world of white secrets carefully guarded" (p. 45). The Daltons have "a big white cat" (p. 49) that later sits in ominous judgment of Bigger as he burns Mary's lifeless body. Seated between Jan and Mary in the Daltons' car, Bigger feels as if he is "sitting between two vast white looming walls" (p. 68). It is the "awesome white blur floating toward him" (p. 85) in the darkness of Mary's room that seals his fate, for in trying to muffle Mary's groans he inadvertently kills her. When Mr. Dalton and Britten first question Bigger about Mary's absence, their faces are "white discs of danger floating still in the air" (p. 146). And when Jan becomes the first white man whom Bigger sees as human, he is like "a particle of white rock" that detaches itself "from that looming mountain of white hate" (p. 268).

The coldness of the white world becomes tangibly present to Bigger in the falling snow that later develops into a blizzard impeding escape and gradually entombing him in its cold white prison. He is frightened when the intensity of the sun makes "the snow leap and glitter and sparkle about him in a world of magic whiteness without sound" (p. 114). While Bigger plans the kidnap note with Bessie, they are surrounded by "white snow and the night" (p. 139). When the snow stops falling, the city is "all white, still" (p. 226). Unable to flee his snowbound South Side prison, Bigger scans the paper to note the progress of the eight thousand white men who are out searching for him in the night. The unsearched area, ironically the "white portion" (p. 230) on the map, is shrinking rapidly. Finally, all that is left to him is a "tiny square of white," and he feels as if he is "gazing down into the barrel of a gun" (p. 239).

The white world is also blind—blind to what does not fit into the pattern of its desires—and it is this blindness that both makes possible and necessitates Bigger's act of rebellion. "They did not want to see what others were doing if that doing did not feed their own desires" (p. 102). Thus Bigger comes to the conclusion: "The thing to do was to act just like others acted, live like they lived, and while they were not looking, do what you wanted" (p. 102). Nevertheless, it is the literal blindness of Mrs. Dalton that forces Bigger to kill Mary; her blindness is, indeed, the immediate cause of the chain of events that seal his fate.

The opposing strand of images, representing the effect that the cold, white world has on Bigger, is composed of imagery of fire, heat and tension. Just before the abortive robbery of Blum's, Bigger experiences a "ball of hot tightness growing larger and heavier in his stomach and chest" (p. 37); his entire body hungers for release, for "something exciting and violent to relieve the tautness" (p. 38). There is "something like hot water bubbling inside of him and trying to come out" (p. 39). When Buddy, his brother, offers help, Bigger's body is "as taut as that of an animal about to leap" (p. 105). While writing the kidnap note, he senses a rising movement in his stomach, "as though he held within the embrace of his bowels the swing of planets through space" (p. 167). The inner tension that seeks release is symbolized throughout the central portion of the narrative by the ominous presence of the furnace in the Dalton basement, with its bed of coals quivering "with molten fury" (p. 89) and casting a huge red shadow against the wall. When his crime is about to be discovered, Bigger becomes the furnace: "He himself was a huge furnace now through which no air could go; and the fear that surged into his stomach, filling him, choking him, was like the fumes of smoke that had belched from the ash bin" (p. 205).

The release that Bigger seeks from the tension created in him by the oppressive white world comes finally through acts of violence—private moments of apocalypse that are simultaneously acts of creation, yielding him a momentary new birth of freedom. "He had murdered," he reflects, "and had created a new life for himself. It was something that was all his own, and it was the first time in his life that he had had anything that others could not take from him" (p. 101). The subsequent plans for drawing the ransom money before the crime can be discovered give his life a definition he had never before experienced. "He moved consciously between two sharply defined poles: he was moving away from the threatening penalty of death, from the death-like times that brought him that tightness and hotness in his chest; and he was moving toward that sense of fulness he had so often but inadequately felt in magazines and movies" (p. 141). After killing Bessie to keep her from talking, he feels "a queer sense of power" (p. 224). The two murders that he has committed seem to be "the most meaningful things that had ever happened to him" (p. 225). And when Reverend Hammond tries to get Bigger to repent, by telling him the purpose of his existence in terms of the creation story from Genesis, Bigger reflects that he had long ago erased that picture from his mind because the white world did not include him in that picture of creation. In order to live, he had had to create "a new world for himself" (p. 264) ; and for this he knows he must die. Having tried to create a life for himself and failed, he looks wistfully in his mind "upon the dark face of ancient waters upon which some spirit had breathed and created him" (p. 255) and yearns for eternal rest.

Max, in his futile courtroom plea for mercy, stressing the condition of oppression that had inevitably brought Bigger to violence, insists again that for Bigger it was not murder, but "an act of *creation*," in fact "the first full act of his life" (p. 366, 364). It is Max, too, who predictably and eloquently asks the question that gives universal apocalyptic significance to the futile necessity of creative violence: "Who knows when another 'accident' involving millions of men will happen, an 'accident' that will be the dreadful day of our doom?" (p. 369). The prophetic message is clear—those who refuse to allow the freedom of individual expression must expect the universial *dies irae* as certainly as night follows day. Max warns that without mercy "this vicious game will roll on, like a bloody river to a bloodier sea" (p. 358).

Paralleling the microcosm of seething tension within Bigger are the macrocosmic images of impending secular doom that build in intensity to the climax of the novel; they simply corroborate Max's prophetic warning. There is the "lightning" of incessant camera flashes, and the "searching knives of light" (p. 248) that pierce the night of the manhunt—suggesting also, no doubt, the flaming sword of the angel who drives Bigger from his brief Eden of personal independence. Bigger wonders whether he is not "a man born for dark doom, an obscene joke happening amid a colossal din of siren screams and white faces and circling lances of light under a cold and silken sky" (p. 256). Disturbing the quiet of the still, white night is a medley of crashing sounds—"horns, sirens, screams" (p. 241). There is fear of massive retaliation or of a black uprising, and during the trial "the rumbling mutter of the vast mob" (p. 345) drifts into the courtroom.

The injustice of Bigger's fate is emphasized by an image of crucifixion at the time of his capture, which for Bigger, because he is black, is the equivalent of death. He is nailed to the cross of the cold, white world: "Two men stretched his arms out, as though about to crucify him; they placed a foot on each of his wrists, making them sink deep down in the snow" (p. 253).

Through his contact with Max, Bigger grows in understanding the general condition of man in a way somewhat reminiscent of the nameless hero of *Invisible Man*—but without the positive tone of the latter. He has a vision in which he sees in succession the world as "a black sprawling prison full of tiny black cells" and then "a strong blinding sun sending hot rays down" to melt away the differences among men—"white men and black men and all men" (pp. 334–35). Max has helped Bigger to realize that in some sense all men are oppressed, and so he asks himself: "Was there some battle everybody was fighting, and he had missed it?" (p. 336). Thus when Bigger says finally, "What I killed for, I *am*!" (pp. 391–92), it is with the ironic realization that his killers will and must say the same thing.

Invisible Man gives definitive modern treatment to the secular symbolism of the last loosing of Satan; *Go Tell It on the Mountain* focuses on the symbolism of new life, but for purposes of irony. Richard Wright employs a double symbolism of catastrophe in his images of fire and ice that represent the opposing factions of a racially divided country. Frost suggests that for destruction ice may be as good as fire; Wright's unambiguous world of icy white domination comes to an end because of the fire of violent passion that it generates in the oppressed.

Wright also uses the imagery of creation. It is not, however, the new heaven and the new earth of the final kingdom; it is a repetition of images from the first creation. The Genesis imagery suggests that Bigger is not regenerated through violence, but is actually born for the first time. More fundamentally still, it is only ironically a creation. Although Bigger feels that he can assert his selfhood only through violence, the self that he has created cannot survive. It is caught up in the viciously circular process of human domination and oppression. Asserting himself in violence, he will be violently suppressed by whites in order that they may maintain their own selfhood. Because the novel was written against white domination of America, it judges primarily the cold, white oppressive world. Wright's judgment, however, yields universal meaning. He seems to be saying also that it is man's lot to try, paradoxically, to survive by violent means—only to fail. The way of oppression leads inevitably to disaster.

These three novels, in the order of their treatment here, represent a sliding scale from the universal appeal of Ellison's parable about man to Wright's intended and realized black protest. For Ellison, modern man, seeking to know who he is, must acknowledge the death in himself as well as in others. Baldwin, eschewing protest and treating instead of the shared experiences of black people, shows the agony and ecstasy of their simplistic faith —a refuge from white oppression and thus an obstacle to progress. Wright portrays unambiguously the tension of the black ghetto surrounded by a white racist world —and the meaning of violence.

From a literary standpoint—and I reflect here what seems to be a consensus of critics—Wright is less successful than either Ellison or Baldwin. One wonders whether this is a judgment based strictly on the merits of his literary craftsmanship or more a reflection of the difficulties involved in writing an artistically successful protest novel. Great literature at any rate seems to thrive on ambiguity, and this is at least one quality that *Native Son* does not possess.

The predominance of apocalyptic imagery in each of these novels can be attributed to a variety of factors, as I observed earlier. According to R. W. B. Lewis, apoc-

alypse is an idiom common to contemporary writers.
Yet even Lewis implies that this is hardly a universal
literary phenomenon. It is, however, consistent and
prominent among these outstanding black novelists,
despite the fact that they represent such a variety of
literary purposes. One is inclined, although aware of the
dangers of psychological criticism, to assert that writers of an oppressed minority will necessarily reflect the
tension that life has habituated them to. And the
greater and more long-standing the frustration they
have known, the less hope their imagination will reflect.

It is not surprising either that only Baldwin employs
specifically Christian images. Here the subject matter,
a realistic portrayal of the ordinary lives of American
Negroes, has governed the flow of his imagery. Reading
the autobiographical notes in *The Fire Next Time*
against the characterization of John Grimes, it seems
clear that the novel itself is highly autobiographical. It
was not long after Baldwin's conversion experience that
he rejected the church because he found no love in it and
because its God was white. For him the church is built
on the three principles of "Blindness, Loneliness, and
Terror, the first principle necessarily and actively culti-
vated in order to deny the two others."[11] His incisive
criticism of white religion adapted to keep black people
"in their place" is a clear indication that Christianity is
for all too many black people an obstacle to progress
and the achievement of even the most basic human
rights. Because Christianity has been such a convenient
tool in the hands of white racists, it is irony, if not jus-

tice, that its sterner eschatology, drained of hope, has become a trumpet of doom for the white dream.

The apocalyptic imagery of these novels wrenches us into the tensions of the last days and imparts a proportionate sense of urgency or despair. Wright, though, has taken us beyond the fright of impending doom. With great clarity and precision, he hammers home the theme that violence is the only possibility for the oppressed, that it is the only way for a black man in America to be creative. The novel, however, does not counsel violence; it simply states a fact.

CHAPTER FIVE

Loss of World in Barth, Pynchon, and Vonnegut:

The Varieties of Humorous Apocalypse

There is a current literary tendency to treat cultural crisis in a humorous vein. But black humor, as the trend is frequently called, it one of those critical categories that has been stretched so far that it has become useless, especially when it groups together such diverse talents as John Barth, Thomas Pynchon, and Kurt Vonnegut, Jr. The very application of a genus always tends, obviously, to obscure the unique richness of the works of the individuals in question; the exaggeration of similarities destroys identity altogether. Black humorists supposedly know what the joke is, and in being able to point it out to us enable us to laugh along with them. But the joke, we are told, is life; the only salvation, laughing.[1]

If this is the essence of black humor, then Barth alone of the three writers under consideration in this chapter is a possible candidate for the title of black humorist. Humorous apocalypse is another critical label used of the same novels, yet in a way that often makes it appear as if black humor and humorous apocalypse are the same. A careful distinction should be made for the sake of diversity of genres and greater accuracy in their application. If humorous apocalypse is defined as imagined catastrophe that nevertheless provokes laughter, then this classification seems initially more appropriate to the writers in question, at least in their works selected for consideration here—Barth's *The End of the Road* (1967), Pynchon's *The Crying of Lot 49* (1966) and Vonnegut's *Cat's Cradle* (1963).

The title of each of these novels is an image of apocalypse. Barth's title speaks for itself. Pynchon's is a latter-day equivalent of the blast of the archangel's trumpet announcing the final revelation, for presumably the collection of stamps at auction as "lot 49" holds the key to the possible revelation of a mysterious web of evil undergirding modern America. And a "cat's cradle," the design made with string, is a symbol of the precarious position of a world victimized by man's absurd pretensions.

Each of the novels has a narrative structure based on the pattern of discovery, and in each case the quest yields apocalyptic meaning. In *The End of the Road*, Jacob Horner is searching for his own identity, and with the help of his existentialist doctor he discovers the dead end that mythotherapy leads to. Oedipa Maas, in *The Crying of Lot 49*, uncovers—possibly—a system of underworld communication, while acting as executrix of Pierce Inverarity's estate. And the narrator of *Cat's Cradle*, researching a book on the atomic bomb, finds out about *ice-nine* and meets the family that sponsors the end of the world.

I

In *The End of the Road*, when Rennie Morgan tells Jacob Horner, "I don't know where all this will lead to,"[2] she indicates an ignorance of direction that Barth has designed his novel to answer. The last word of the novel, "Terminal," pinpoints that answer perfectly. *The End of the Road* is concerned with the loss of world that is common to all apocalyptic writing. What comes to such a certain end here is the world of absolutes that Jacob Horner and Joe Morgan live in. Although the Doctor's absolute would seem to be the most destructive of them all, his world does not apparently end; it simply relocates itself. But the reason why he does not lose his world is a significant aspect of the apocalyptic meaning of the novel and one that we will investigate in detail later.

There are many references to absolutes and levels of absolutes in the novel; I will be concerned principally with the absolutes that the central characters themselves describe by way of self-analysis. Horner's absolute, which he calls "articulation," and Morgan's principle of consistency are subordinate in importance to the Doctor's absolute—existential therapy. These absolutes, such as they are, are defined within the context of the two principal conflicts in the novel: Morgan and Horner over Rennie, and Morgan and the Doctor over Horner's selfhood. The latter struggle is more typical of the meaning of the novel, and the image that Horner offers of himself struggling is Laocoön.

The Laocoön on Horner's mantlepiece is not only the central object in his apartment but also the principal symbol in the novel. Horner awakens each day to its "voiceless groan" (p. 21). At the end of his story, in the "raggedness" and "incompleteness" of Rennie's death, Horner realizes that his paralysis makes him like Laocoön; he reflects: "My limbs were bound like Laocoön's —by the serpents Knowledge and Imagination, which, grown great in the fullness of time, no longer tempt but annihilate" (p. 196). In the dualistic game for control of Jacob's self, Joe Morgan and the Doctor represent Knowledge and Imagination respectively; they are also God and Satan, just as Morgan and Horner represent God and Satan in the struggle for Rennie, who is the soul of man. Horner renders this analogy explicit: "Joe was The Reason, or Being (I was using Rennie's cosmos); I was the Unreason, or Not-Being; and the two of us were fighting without quarter for possession of Rennie, like God and Satan for the soul of Man" (p. 129). Although Horner in his usual manner immediately retracts what he has just stated, claiming that this "pretty ontological Manichaeism would certainly stand no close examination" (p. 129), there can be no doubt that the pattern of relationships in the novel is antithetical. We are witnessing the parody of some primal, cosmic struggle for the re-creation of man. But since absolutes by definition do not yield, there is no new life.

Jacob's personality alternates between the manic and utter moodlessness. He has a dream in which he must learn the weather prediction for the following day. After many futile efforts to discover the forecast, he finally reaches the Weather Bureau, only to receive the answer: "There isn't going to be any weather tomorrow" (p. 36). Although he relates the dream to his periods "without any mood at all" (p. 36), there is in it also a mild apocalyptic foreshadowing of the conclusion of his story. This alternation between the manic and moodlessness is reflected in his supposed absolute, which is articulation; for only Jacob Horner can express an absolute with one breath and deny it with the next. After a disturbing conversation with Joe Morgan, Horner realizes his absolute:

> Articulation! There, by Joe, was *my* absolute, if I could be said to have one. At any rate, it is the only thing I can think of about which I ever had, with any frequency at all, the feelings one usually has for one's absolutes. To turn experience into speech—that is, to classify, to categorize, to conceptualize, to grammarize, to syntactify it—is always a betrayal of experience, a falsification of it; but only so betrayed can it be dealt with at all, and only in so dealing with it did I ever feel a man, alive and kicking. It is therefore that, when I had cause to think about it at all, I responded to this precise falsification, this adroit, careful myth-making, with all the upsetting exhilaration of any artist at his work. When my mythoplastic razors were sharply honed, it was unparalleled sport to lay about with them, to have at reality.
>
> In other senses, of course, I don't believe this at all.

Later, in telling his whole story to the Doctor, Jacob admits: "It was enormously refreshing to articulate it all" (p. 178).

Yet in the final analysis Horner knows that his real problem is "that it was never very much of a chore for [him], at various times, to maintain with perfectly equal unenthusiasm contradictory, or at least polarized, opinions at once on a given subject" (p. 120). The chaos of Jacob's life is accentuated by the advice the Doctor gives him: to counteract the paralysis that he experiences, he is encouraged to act impulsively, to "join things" (p. 85); he is told to teach prescriptive grammar because it involves "no optional situations" (p. 5).

Joe Morgan's absolute is the professed absence of absolutes. He tells Jacob, "Less-than-absolutes are all we've got" (pp. 42–43). The troublesome fallacy in a world without absolutes, as Joe sees it, is "that because a value isn't intrinsic, objective, and absolute, it somehow isn't *real*" (pp. 44–45). Even though nothing is ultimately defensible for Joe, "a man can act coherently; he can act in ways that he can explain, if he wants to" (p. 47). Thus, Joe goes on to explain, "the only demonstrable index to a man's desires is his acts, when you're speaking of past time: what a man did is what he wanted to do" (p. 49).

"Living coherently" becomes for Joe as rigid an absolute as anyone could live by. Since Joe prides himself on understanding his wife, he concludes that if he knows what she does he will also know why. Not only is Joe deluded in assuming knowledge of his wife (he is at a total loss to know why she has had the affair with Horner), there are also absurd inconsistencies in his practice of consistency. Supposedly at work diligently on his dissertation, which would be in keeping with the

coherence of his public life, Joe is observed surreptitiously
by Horner and Rennie; he is preening himself before a
mirror, and later he masturbates. The contrast of public
attitude and secret action is patently absurd. Joe's
obstinate insistence that the reason for Rennie's infidelity
is discoverable contributes as much as anything to the
tragic outcome of her relationship with Horner. Jacob
reflects on the demoralizing effect of dealing with a man
who will "unhesitatingly act upon the extremest limits
of his ideas" (p. 155). Granting at first that Joe is "noble
as the dickens," Horner concludes that he is monomaniacal "in the delusion that intelligence will solve all
problems" (p. 123).

The Doctor, committed to mythotherapy as the ultimate of therapies, manifests the severe limitations of
existentialism. Mythotherapy is based on the supposi-
tion that "the same life lends itself to any number of
stories" (p. 5). In more technical language these are its
two assumptions as the Doctor sees them: "That human
existence precedes human essence, if either of the two
terms really signifies anything; and that a man is free
not only to choose his own essence but to change it at
will." The Doctor assures Jacob, "Those are both good
existentialist premises, and whether they're true or
false is of no concern to us— they're *useful* in your case"
(p. 88). The Doctor, though, proves that he knows
Horner as little as Morgan knows his wife. Horner feels
guilt about his tragic involvement with the Morgans,
and the Doctor must finally tell him: "Mythotherapy
would have kept you out of any involvement, if you'd
practiced it assiduously the whole time. Actually you did

practice it, but like a ninny you gave yourself the wrong part. Even the villain's role would have been all right, if you'd been an out-and-out villain with no regrets! But you've made yourself a penitent when it's too late to repent" (p. 180).

The Doctor's philosophy is responsible for Jacob's loss of world; there is also considerable evidence that he epitomizes the last loosing of Satan before the final cataclysm. His imagination, that could possibly have been used to support Horner, serves only to enslave him. He is "a Negro doctor with an all-white clientele" (p. 185), who remains nameless throughout. The Progress and Advice Room at the Doctor's Remobilization Farm is ironically all white: the walls are flat white, the windows covered by white venetian blinds, and the only furniture in the room is "two straight-backed white wooden chairs" (p. 1). The Doctor wears "a white medical-looking jacket" (p. 79). There is a surrealism in his presentation that fits the apocalyptic imagination perfectly.

That the Doctor is a con man seems clear from the fact that his unorthodox practices require him to move frequently and quickly from place to place. When Horner goes to the Doctor to ask him to perform Rennie's abortion, he is making final preparations to move from Maryland to Pennsylvania. Large corrugated boxes are in the entrance hall; the reception room is lined with "rolled carpets, disarranged furniture, and more paper boxes" (p. 177). The Doctor agrees to perform the abortion on the condition that Horner will give him all the money he has and move with them to Pennsylvania. He claims to want Horner on hand twenty-four hours a day for therapy; the second reason, which seems more realistic, is that he will need a young man to do manual labor "while the new farm is being set up" (p. 182). On the appointed day, Horner is to meet Mrs. Dockey, the Doctor's assistant, at the bus terminal. There is a stark reality about the description of the abortion and an emptiness in the concluding events that contribute greatly toward interpreting the Doctor as demonic. Horner's world disintegrates so completely that there is nothing left for him to do but to go to the terminal.

In the typology of apocalypse, *The End of the Road* is more explicit about the reasons for the end than in the imagination of the end itself, although this too is described clearly enough as the ultimate absence of alternative. A type of humorous apocalypse that is secular in imagination, it projects a loss of world which results from the conflict of absolutes. Existentialism, as we have seen, is perhaps the most specific secular idealogy judged conducive to disaster. The Doctor, whose victory leads to the end of the road, is a con man, the secular analogue of Satan loose for the last time. No alternative to disaster is offered, yet it is cynicism or frustration rather than despair that prompts the vision without hope.

II

In *The Crying of Lot 49*, the declaration of Pierce Inverarity's will initiates a process of discovery that leads Oedipa Maas to the very brink of significant revelation. Prior to the announcement of the will, Oedipa imagines herself a Rapunzel-like "prisoner among the pines and salt fogs of Kinneret."[3] Pierce had indeed asked her to let down her hair, but somehow everything that transpired between them during their brief affair "had really never escaped the confinement of that tower" (p. 10). Escape from the tower, if it is escape at all, begins with her unavoidable involvement in the litigation of Inverarity's estate. Confused about why she should be named as executrix, she seems at first not even to be interested in what she may find out; but "as things developed, she was to have all manner of revelations" (p. 9).

The mood of unfolding revelation is the central motif ◄ of the novel. As soon as Oedipa sees San Narciso, the site of Inverarity's home and headquarters, "the ordered swirl of houses and streets" (p. 13) of that southern California city reminds her of the printed circuit of a transistor radio. In both patterns she could perceive "a hieroglyphic sense of concealed meaning, of an intent to communicate" (p. 13). The appearance of patterns in the world of artifacts is consistently associated with the suggestion of revelation. Oedipa's first view of San Narciso is a "religious instant": "So in her first minute of San Narciso, a revelation also trembled just past the threshold of her understanding" (p. 13). A television commercial for Fangoso Lagoons, one of Inverarity's interests, showing the lacy pattern of canals and streets has this effect on Oedipa: "Some immediacy was there again, some promise of hierophany: printed circuit, gently curving streets, private access to water . . ." (p. 18).

Oedipa comes to consider her affair with Metzger, the coexecutor of the estate, as the logical starting point of

her escape from the tower "if one object behind her discovery of what she was to label the Tristero System or
often only The Tristero . . . were to bring to an end her
encapsulation in her tower" (p. 28). She is haunted by
the way the pieces seem to fit together logically; it was
"as if . . . there were revelation in progress all around
her" (p. 28). She suspects that "a plunge toward dawn
indefinite black hours long would indeed be necessary
before The Tristero could be revealed in its terrible
nakedness" (p. 36). Later, the revelations related to The
Tristero seem "to come crowding in exponentially" (p.
58). "Because of other revelations, . . . a pattern was
beginning to emerge" (p. 64). Yet, despite the proliferation of clues, ambiguity plagues the process of revelation: "Oedipa wondered whether, at the end of this
(if it were supposed to end), she too might not be left
with only compiled memories of clues, announcements,
intimations, but never the central truth itself, which
must somehow each time be too bright for her memory
to hold" (p. 69). Again, "she wondered if the gemlike
'clues' were only some kind of compensation. To make
up for her having lost the direct, epileptic Word, the cry
that might abolish the night" (p. 87).

The expectation of revelation is supported by the
actual unfolding of the narrative. The process of anticipated revelation has two moments: The first involves
the proliferation of evidence relating to The Tristero;
the second, the intensification of expectation resulting
from the mysterious disappearance of informants.

The revelation is all related to The Tristero, and
"much of the revelation was to come through the stamp

collection Pierce had left" (p. 28). Oedipa receives a
letter from her husband, Mucho Maas, with a government advertisement next to the cancellation that reads:
"REPORT ALL OBSCENE MAIL TO YOUR POTSMASTER"
(p. 30). "Potsmaster" is apparently not a misprint. It
was probably the same evening, Oedipa is not sure, that
she and Metzger discovered The Scope, a bar near Inverarity's Yoyodyne plant. On the wall of the ladies' room,
Oedipa finds a message for those "interested in sophisticated fun"; they are to contact Kirby "through
WASTE only" (p. 34). Beneath the notice is a symbol
that Oedipa later identifies as a muted post horn. It is
at The Scope that she meets Mike Fallopian who is
"doing a history of private mail delivery in the U.S.,
attempting to link the Civil War to the postal reform
movement that had begun around 1845" (p. 35). Thus
began for Oedipa "the languid, sinister blooming of The
Tristero" (p. 36).

Manny Di Presso, Metzger's actor-lawyer friend,
announces one day at Fangoso Lagoons that he has a
client, named Tony Jaguar, who is suing Inverarity's
estate because Pierce allegedly had never paid him for a
shipment of bones. Inverarity owned 51 percent of the
charcoal filter process linked with Beaconsfield Ciga-
rettes. Jaguar had harvested the bones from the bottom
of Lago di Pietà in Italy; they had apparently belonged
to American soldiers killed during World War II and
interred in the lake by the Germans. The mention of
bodies buried in a lake reminds a girl friend of one of the
Paranoids (a rock group that follows Oedipa around)
of a Jacobean revenge play that they had seen, *The Cour-*

ier's Tragedy by Richard Wharfinger. And then the
pieces of the puzzle begin to fit together rapidly. In the
play, which Oedipa attends as soon as possible, the "Trystero" assassins massacre the Faggian Guard and throw
their bodies into a lake, in apparent vendetta against the
Thurn and Taxis postal monopoly. The assassins appear
in a fashion reminiscent of the Furies, dark balancers of
the scale of cosmic justice: "Suddenly, in lithe and terrible silence, with dancers' grace, three figures, long-
limbed, effeminate, dressed in black tights, leotards and
gloves, black silk hose pulled over their faces, come
capering on stage and stop. . . . Their faces behind the
stockings are shadowy and deformed" (p. 51). It is clear
that "whoever they were their aim was to mute the
Thurn and Taxis post horn" (p. 70). The post horn with
a single loop was on the Thurn and Taxis coat of arms;
and so the line announcing the massacre reads: "And
Tacit lies the gold once-knotted horn" (p. 52). The
WASTE symbol that Oedipa had discovered was of course
the muted post horn.

Mr. Thoth, a senior citizen at Inverarity's Vesperhaven House, whose grandfather had ridden for the
Pony Express during the days of the gold rush, shows
Oedipa a signet ring with the WASTE symbol on it. His
grandfather had cut it from the finger of one of the
"Indians who wore black feathers, the Indians who
weren't Indians" (p. 67)—who fought the Pony
Express apparently because of a longstanding vendetta
against the established postal system. Touring Inverarity's Yoyodyne plant, Oedipa notices an employee, Stanley Koteks, doodling a muted post horn. He informs her

that what she calls the WASTE symbol is "an acronym, not 'waste'" (p. 63) and tells her about inventors who were raised on the myth of the American Inventor and then grew up to discover that "they had to sign over all their rights to a monster like Yoyodyne" (p. 64). Koteks apparently uses the WASTE system to contact John Nefastis, inventor of a machine that "contained an honest-to-God Maxwell's Demon" (p. 62).

A pattern had all but emerged. Under the symbol in her memo book, Oedipa wrote: "*Shall I project a world?* If not project then at least flash some arrow on the dome to skitter among constellations and trace out your Dragon, Whale, Southern Cross" (p. 59). These are the facts she had amassed if indeed they could be called that: "[The Tristero] had opposed the Thurn and Taxis postal system in Europe; its symbol was a muted post horn; sometime before 1853 it had appeared in America and fought the Pony Express and Wells Fargo, either as outlaws in black, or disguised as Indians; and it survived today, in California, serving as a channel of communication for those of unorthodox sexual persuasion, inventors who believed in the reality of Maxwell's Demon, possibly her own husband, Mucho Maas" (p. 80).

Then Oedipa wanders in despair through San Francisco and spends "the rest of the night finding the image of the Trystero[4] post horn" (p. 86). On the back of a bus seat she finds "the post horn with the legend DEATH. But unlike WASTE, somebody had troubled to write in, in pencil: DON'T EVER ANTAGONIZE THE HORN" (p. 90). When at last, under the elevated freeway, Oedipa finds her first WASTE mailbox, the humorous irony of the reve-

lation is almost anticlimactic. It is "a can with a swinging trapezoidal top, the kind you throw trash in: old and
green, nearly four feet high. On the swinging part were
handpainted the initials w.a.s.t.e. She had to look
closely to see the periods between the letters" (p. 96).

A major parody of the novel deals with textual criticism. Emory Bortz is an authority on the Wharfinger
play, and Oedipa feels rightly that she must investigate
this source as deeply as possible. The version that Randolph Driblette uses the night Oedipa is present, the one
that mentions The Tristero by name, is a pornographic
Vatican edition attributed to the Scurvhamites, an ultra-
Puritan sect that apparently wanted to degrade the play
as a moral example for its members. The Scurvhamites,
according to Bortz, were dualists who believed that all
evil is the work of "the brute Other." Apparently they
felt "Trystero would symbolize the Other quite well"
(p. 117).

A final, and seemingly conclusive, piece is added to
the puzzle when Genghis Cohen, "the most eminent
philatelist in the L. A. area" (p. 68), gets in the mail "an
old American stamp, bearing the device of the muted
post horn"; its motto "we await silent tristero's
empire" (p. 127) reveals at last the meaning of the
mysterious acronym. Despite the fact that the contemporary significance of The Tristero is still obscure for
Oedipa, it is abundantly clear to her that "every access
route to The Tristero [can] be traced also back to the
Inverarity estate. . . . Meaning what? That Bortz, along
with Metzger, Cohen, Driblette, Koteks, the tatooed
sailor in San Francisco, the w.a.s.t.e. carriers she'd

seen—that all of them were Pierce Inverarity's men? *Bought*? Or loyal, for free, for fun, to some grandiose practical joke he'd cooked up, all for her embarrassment, or terrorizing, or moral improvement?" (pp. 127–28). Regardless of how it is linked with Inverarity, The Tristero—either hired by him or independent and cooperating—is indubitably his.

Yet just as a significant pattern begins to emerge, Oedipa loses, one by one, her best sources of information. And so the second moment of the revelatory process commences—an intensification of the expectation of revelation. Oedipa's psychiatrist, Dr. Hilarius, pursued by Israelis, goes mad. Her husband, Mucho, is on LSD, groping "like a child further and further into the rooms and endless rooms of the elaborate candy house of himself" (p. 114). Metzger, the co-executor, has eloped with a depraved fifteen-year-old; and Randolph Driblette walks to his death in the Pacific. Zapf's Used Books, where Oedipa had discovered a copy of Wharfinger's play, has been burned to the ground, reportedly by Zapf himself. Oedipa begins to fear for Emory Bortz and Genghis Cohen "in view of what was happening to everyone else she knew" (p. 120). Suddenly she becomes "reluctant about following up anything"; she feels certain that if she returned to Vesperhaven House to see Mr. Thoth, "she would find that he too had died" (p. 124).

John W. Hunt, who has written perhaps the most thorough analysis of the novel to date, is less subtle in his interpretation of the ending than the conclusion deserves. Commenting on Pynchon as a novelist, he makes this general observation:

> Pynchon, too, is a child of his time who finds the absurd nature of life something with which he begins rather than ends. . . . We experience this fragmented world as absurd, he seems to say, and we should leave it at that; attempts at rational connection should be avoided not because they are unsuccessful but because they are too successful. Pynchon focuses upon the maddeningly elusive *apparent* connections which seem to threaten the disconnections with which his characters have learned to live.[5]

Hunt summarizes the ambiguity of the ending of *The Crying of Lot 49* in this way: "If this world is not the fragmented, disconnected thing it appears to be—dull, out of focus, void of meaning, and leading to death—then its apparent discontinuity is actually held together by a secret, elusive, and transcendent meaning the knowledge of which leads to madness."[6]

After the experience of the gradual disclosure of information suggesting a pattern of underworld communication, intensified by the sudden and unaccountable disappearance of her best sources, Oedipa herself lists the alternatives; there are four, "these symmetrical four": Either she has stumbled upon "a secret richness and concealed density of dream; onto a network by which X number of Americans are truly communicating whilst reserving their lies, recitations of routine, arid betrayals of spiritual poverty, for the official government delivery system" (p. 128), or she is hallucinating the existence of such a network. The third possibility is that she has discovered a plot mounted against her, financed by the

Inverarity estate, "so expensive and elaborate, . . . so laby- (3)
rinthine that it must have meaning beyond just a practical joke" (p. 128); or she is genuinely paranoid in (4)
"fantasying some such plot" (p. 128). San Narciso,
whatever its secret meaning may be, is America:
"[Oedipa] had dedicated herself, weeks ago, to making
sense of what Inverarity had left behind, never suspect-
ing that the legacy was America" (p. 134).

John Hunt's interpretation is less subtle than the ending deserves because the possibility of the genuine
disclosure of transcendent meaning is quite distinct
from the hypothesis of madness; there seems to be little
warrant for suggesting as Hunt does that the "transcen- ⁷
dent meaning . . . leads to madness."⁷ James Young, on
the other hand, in commenting on the significance of
Oedipa's name, seems to have found too little meaning.
He suggests that Oedipa Maas means "not so much 'more
than Oedipus' as too much, the woman seeking for the
cause of the plague of the city for which she has been
named coexecutor."⁸ (The city of course is Inverarity's
San Narciso.) Young goes on to say that Oedipa is only
ironically Oedipus because she comes up with no solution. She does, however, as we have seen, enumerate four
alternatives, one of which she—and the reader through
her—expects definitely to be disclosed with the crying of lot 49. It is precisely at this point that the
commentators seem to have missed the implications of
apocalypse in the novel; there is a decided inclination
toward the expectation of unambiguous revelation, and
the only solution for Oedipa is to wait.

The Tristero system, insofar as it suggests a conspiracy

for evil of some sort, would remain simply an idea of Oedipa's if it were not for the second moment of revelation that I described. The actual curious disappearance ⌐of Oedipa's sources seems more than coincidental. That the auction is important to the meaning of The Tristero is clear from the novel's structure and the significance of the title, and the references to the auction are consistently sinister. Genghis Cohen hears that there is to be a "book bidder" on lot 49, the title under which Inverarity's Tristero stamp collection is to be sold. A book bidder remains anonymous; the air of mystery surrounding him suggests that he "wants to keep evidence that Tristero exists out of unauthorized hands" (p. 132). As the time for the auction draws near, Oedipa experiences the "waiting above all" (p. 136). Her four alternatives are reduced to the latter two, which she keeps reviewing for herself in various ways: "Behind the hieroglyphic streets there would either be a transcendent meaning, or only the earth. . . . Ones and zeroes. . . . Either Oedipa in the orbiting ecstasy of a true paranoia, or a real Tristero" (pp. 136–37).

And then the day of the auction comes, and the sense of expectation reaches apocalyptic intensity. The auction room seems more like a tribunal of judgment. Loren Passerine, "the finest auctioneer in the West" (p. 137), "hovered like a puppet-master, his eyes bright, his smile practiced and relentless" (p. 138). The mysterious bidder has, at the last minute, decided to attend in person; Oedipa scans the room, "trying to guess which one was her target, her enemy, perhaps her proof" (p. 138). Everyone in the room seems to be a Tristero assassin:

"The men inside the auction room wore black mohair
and had pale, cruel faces" (p. 137).

The door to the room is locked, and Passerine spreads
"his arms in a gesture that seemed to belong to the priest-
hood of some remote culture; perhaps to a descending
angel" (p. 138). It is still, just before the conclusion of
the novel, simply a gesture belonging "perhaps" to a
descending angel. Immediately afterwards comes the
final unrelieved note of apocalyptic anticipation: "The
auctioneer cleared his throat. Oedipa settled back, to
await the crying of lot 49" (p. 138). The name Oepida,
too, supports the expectation of the revelation of meaning. Oedipus symbolizes the discovery of evil in oneself;
this implication adds a dimension of meaning that even
Oedipa had not considered. She is Oedipus at least in the
sense that her quest for meaning has been serious.

In the symbolism of apocalypse, *The Crying of Lot 49*
converts the moment of warning prior to disaster into
the impersonal category of anticipated revelation. Even
though the content of the revelation remains ambiguous,
the imminent expectation of it does not. As humorous
apocalypse, however, it is open to the possibility that our
worst fears may not materialize. America is our legacy;
it is also, perhaps, the name of our disease. We await the
revelation of its true meaning. There is thus a basic
humanity in the modesty of Pynchon's ambiguous
statement of possibilities.

III

Kurt Vonnegut is definitely not a black humorist, at
least as defined earlier in this chapter. As a novelist, he

is sympathetic to the method, rather than the philosophy, of Sherman Krebbs in *Cat's Cradle*. Krebbs is the nihilist who introduces himself as the "National Chairman of Poets and Painters for Immediate Nuclear War."[9] Jonah, the narrator, loans Krebbs his New York apartment and returns from a trip to find it demolished. He confesses that Krebb's action certainly discouraged him from accepting nihilism as a philosophy. Krebbs is, in the language of Bokonon, a *"wrang-wrang, . . .* a person who steers people away from a line of speculation by reducing that line, with the example of the *wrang-wrang's* own life, to an absurdity" (p. 59).

Although, according to Bokonon, a *wrang-wrang* scarcely acts as a conscious *reductio ad absurdum*, the writer who shows the absurd conclusion of a course of action knows what he is about. The black humorist shows us the absurdity of the conclusion, but invites us simply to laugh at the inevitable. There is, it seems to me, considerable evidence that Vonnegut would steer us from one course of action because he has something better in mind, although there is a marked inclination of his imagination to dwell on the limitations of the possibilities that lie before us.

Vonnegut belongs to a purer strain of apocalyptic writers, a tradition that imagines the worst because it believes in something better. Vonnegut's apocalypse is humorous, yet nonetheless genuinely human and hopeful because his imagination clearly conceives of alternatives to catastrophe, however limited those alternatives may be. He offers us modes of action rather than climates of beatitude. Vonnegut as *wrang-wrang* consistently maintains an apocalyptic tone in his unambiguous criticism of society; the alternative to the course that he would steer us from is not always equally clear.

Cat's Cradle is set in a future which in many ways is like our present except that the world is ripe for destruction. It is a novel about "the day the world ended," which is actually the title of the book that the narrator sets out to write. *The Day the World Ended*, however, was supposed to be a Christian account of what important Americans like Dr. Felix Hoenikker, one of the bomb's inventors, were doing on the day the atomic bomb fell on Hiroshima; whereas *Cat's Cradle* becomes a Bokononist account of the way the whole world actually does end.

Bokonon is the pronunciation given the name Johnson in the English dialect of San Lorenzo, a small island dictatorship in the Caribbean. And Johnson is the surname of a black Episcopalian from Tobago who with Earl McCabe, a United States marine deserter, attempted to convert the island of San Lorenzo into a utopia. Johnson had for some time been developing the conviction that "something was trying to get him somewhere for some reason" (p. 76), so when he and McCabe were grounded on San Lorenzo while trying to reach Miami they decided to take control of the pitiful island. The success of their experiment was built on the principle of dynamic tension between religion and government. Bokonon had actually gotten his idea of "pitting good against evil, and . . . keeping the tension between the two high at all times" (p. 74) from a Charles Atlas mail-order muscle building school. So Bokonon allowed himself to be outlawed, and the practice of his religion, which sanctioned the tension, to be a capital offense, punishable by the hook. Bokononism was outlawed for the obvious reason that its paraphrase of Jesus' exhortation to render to Caesar goes like this: "Pay no attention to Caesar. Caesar doesn't have the slightest idea what's *really* going on" (p. 73). Yet everyone, including the dictator, continued to practice Bokononism privately.

Bokonon's sense of being led somewhere by someone for something provoked the formulation of one of the major tenets of his religion, the belief "that humanity is organized into teams, teams that do God's Will without ever discovering what they are doing" (p. 11). One's team is called a *karass*. When Bokonon writes that "man created the checkerboard; God created the *karass*," he means that "a *karass* ignores national, institutional, occupational, familial, and class boundaries" (p. 12). One is not forbidden, moreover, to "discover the limits of his *karass* and the nature of the work God Almighty has had it do" (pp. 12–13); Bokonon simply observes that all "such investigations are bound to be incomplete" (p. 13). It is in seeking to research his book *The Day the World Ended* that Jonah discovers Bokononism, converts, and finally realizes what his "*karass* has been up to" (p. 190). Thus *Cat's Cradle* becomes a novel of the discovery of purpose, and the purpose itself revealed through the humorous interplay of science and religion is at best darkly whimsical.

Researching his book, Jonah also discovers that before Felix Hoenikker died he had invented *ice-nine*, a crystal with a melting point of one hundred and thirty degrees Fahrenheit, capable actually of freezing over the entire world, but mercifully developed simply to solidify swamps for invading Marines. While in Ilium making this cheerful discovery, Jonah has his first "sudden, very personal shove in the direction of Bokononism" (p. 53) when he sees a stone angel under mistletoe in a tombstone salesroom. This *vin-dit*, as the shove is called, is also his first hint about the purpose of his *karass*. At the end of the book, which is also the end of the world, Jonah dreams of climbing Mount McCabe "with some magnificent symbol and planting it there" (p. 190). He realizes that his *karass* has been working "night and day for maybe half a million years to get [him] up that mountain" (p. 190). It is Bokonon himself, sitting on a rock and composing the final sentence of *The Books of Bokonon*, his feet frosty with *ice-nine*, who supplies the appropriate symbol. Jonah reads this on a piece of paper Bokonon hands him: "If I were a younger man, I would write a history of human stupidity; and I would climb to the top of Mount McCabe and lie down on my back with my history for a pillow; and I would take from the ground some of the blue-white poison that makes statues of men; and I would make a statue of myself, lying on my back, grinning horribly, and thumbing my nose at You Know Who" (p. 191).

The absurdity of a world that destroys itself trying to make war easier and of a religion that professes belief in designed frustration is laid before us with the determined genius of a *wrang-wrang*. Robert Scholes sums up his reading of Vonnegut's comment on science and religion in this interesting aphorism: "As the scientist finds the truth that kills, the prophet looks for a saving lie."[10] On the day the bomb fell on Hiroshima, Felix Hoenikker was making a cat's cradle with a piece of string from the manuscript of a convict's novel about the end of the world; the convict had wanted Felix's advice about what sort of explosives to use. Bokonon insists, moreover, that everything in his books, and therefore certainly in his religion, is *foma*, that is to say, lies. Yet despite the insane scientists and the perpetrators of deliberate lies, it is hard to accept a reading of the novel that ends with the black humorist hypothesis and nothing else, even though the purpose of Jonah's *karass* is clearly sketched in the image of a black joke.

Scholes sees black humor, strangely, as a "sign of life and health,"[11] yet his understanding of the ending of this novel involves the acceptance of life as a joke. The best response to life, he writes, is "neither acquiescence nor bitterness. It is first of all a matter of perception. One must 'get' the joke. Then one must demonstrate his awareness by playing one's role in the joke in such a way as to turn the humor back on the joker or cause it to diffuse itself harmlessly on the whole group which has participated in the process of the joke."[12] Even genial nose-thumbing at God seems somehow to be less than enough. Vonnegut has not simply imagined the end as a joke because the insanity of our pretensions must necessarily lead to destruction. His brilliant imagination yields much more here in the way of meaning.

It is true that the Fourteenth Book of Bokonon— entitled "What Can a Thoughtful Man Hope for Mankind on Earth, Given the Experience of the Past Million Years?"—consists of only one word: "Nothing" (p.

164). Such a statement is of course unredemptively pessimistic if one ignores the humorous context; it is also, as an observation about reality, like everything else in Bokononism—a lie. Despite the *foma* one still feels certain that Vonnegut, like the Bokononists, holds at least one thing sacred, and that is man—"just man" (p. 143). Not the man of pretenses who brings the world to destruction, but the man who realizes his extreme limitations, who acknowledges in the words of a Bokonon calypso that "we do . . . what we must . . . muddily do . . . until we bust"(p. 178). In the last rites of Bokononism, man confesses that he is the "sitting-up mud" God made.

It is the "cruel paradox" of Bokononism though, summed up in the couplet about midgets, that ironically enough reveals Vonnegut's hope as well as its limits. The couplet goes: "Midget, midget, midget, how he struts and winks, / For he knows a man's as big as what he hopes and thinks!" (p. 189). The paradox, according to the narrator, consists in "the heartbreaking necessity of lying about reality, and the heartbreaking impossibility of lying about it" (p. 189). Prescinding from the *foma*, we realize that the only hope for man is that he will not lie, that he will accept the fact that he is a moral midget. It is absolutized hope, utopian greed, and absurd pretense that have made the world a "cat's cradle"; and if man does not limit his perspective, "down will come cray-dull, catsy and all" (p. 18).

The destruction of the world by *ice-nine* is in Vonnegut's imagination the logical, though humorously conceived, conclusion of the process of technological expansion, inexorable only if its pretensions are not realized and curtailed. It is the same apocalyptic warning that Loren Eiseley sounds in *The Unexpected Universe*:

> Increasingly, there is but one way into the future: the technological way. The frightening aspect of this situation lies in the constriction of human choice. Western technology has released irrevocable forces, and the one world that has been talked about so glibly is simply a distraught conformity produced by the centripetal forces of Western society. So great is its power over men that any other solution, any other philosophy, is silenced. Men, unknowingly, and whether for good or ill, appear to be making their last decisions about human destiny.[13]

And William Lynch, attempting a new image of the secular, insists that "the history we are so afraid of is a creation of man."[14] The modern secular project, characterized as "technology," has issued in the proliferation of the nonhuman elements that plague our society.

Vonnegut offers us some alternative, however slim, to the path of disaster that we seem consistently to prefer. The world would definitely be easier on people if only we could realize and accept the limitations imposed upon us by existence and by our own innate tendencies and past follies. The norm for judging our actions is whether they reflect a genuine sensitivity to man. Man is sacred, and he must be loved simply because he is a man. And since we are what we pretend to be, Vonnegut seems to be saying, we must be very careful about our hopes and expectations for ourselves and others. We must realize our infinite capacity for harming others, and so our approach to others must always be characterized by respect for their human dignity.

In the final analysis, regardless how insistently and apocalyptically Vonnegut may emphasize the confinement of the human capacity for good, there are possibilities. Thus, in this sequence of contemporary novels, *Cat's Cradle* clearly represents the most humane and hopeful imagination. Ironically, its concentration on the design of the end is a gently humorous program for a new and less pretentious beginning. The reasons for its imagined apocalypse are patent: the pastiche of uncontrolled invention and absolutized religion. Bokononism, cutting religion and man down to size, is the contour of our hope. And if the hope is slender, it is nevertheless genuine.

That these three novels can be classified as humorous is of course a general observation that needs some qualification. Pynchon and Vonnegut offer a kind of gently humorous satire of the madness of modern American society that hardly anyone could miss and certainly no one would be offended by. The humor of *The End of the Road* is of a far more subtle variety. In fact, it seems quite possible that the novel can be read so completely on the literal level that the humor would be missed altogether. Herbert Smith's observation that *The End of the Road* represents "a magnificent parody of the banal love-triangle novel"[15] is a judgment that is not altogether borne out by the evidence of the novel. The humor lies precisely in the contrast that Smith discerns between the level of the love story and the ethical positions that the characters so patently represent, but that this contrast is consistent throughout the novel is a contention that is hard to substantiate. When the realistic level of the novel cannot be taken as anything other than serious—as is the case with the ending—it may simply be a defect of execution rather than of intention.

Despite the humor, the sense of loss of world is acutely present in this contemporary apocalyptic literature. In *The End of the Road* existentialism in the guise of mythotherapy is reduced to an absurdity; if pursued as an absolute, existentialism leads literally to the end of the road. *The Crying of Lot 49* presents the whole of modern America neatly packaged in Pierce Inverarity's San Narciso—the madness of its freeways, the artificiality of its architecture, the sheer absurdity of its social groupings, the emptiness of its scholarship. What has been lost is the possibility, perhaps, of viewing the world as anything other than a circuit set in evil. And Vonnegut in *Cat's Cradle* treats us to an imaginative view of the outcome of our insane pretensions, both technological and religious, asking us to thumb our noses at the image of ourselves we call progress and God.

CHAPTER SIX

Types of Apocalypse in the American Novel

The task of this concluding chapter is twofold: to discern if possible the historical phases of American literary apocalypse disclosed in these twelve representative novels and to expand the typology of apocalypse, projected in chapter 1, to include the variations and innovations analyzed here. This second task will obviously involve determining the possible indebtedness of American authors to the classical symbolisms of apocalypse.

I

The authors whose works I have analyzed critically reflect modes of apocalyptic reaction to three different phases of the American experience. The first phase includes Hawthorne, Melville, and Twain; their apocalypse represents primarily a reaction against the romanticism and liberalism of nineteenth-century American thought. Faulkner, West, and O'Connor are typical of the second phase, which is less a specific reaction against the prevailing culture than an indication of the continuing concern of our great apocalyptic writers for exposing the perennial weaknesses of man. There is nevertheless an emphasis on the individual in their works that reflects the general introversion of American life during the first part of this century. The third phase, including both the black novelists and the humorous apocalyptists of chapters 4 and 5, is confined to the contemporary period. The genuine loss of world that their novels reflect is both national and universal in scope; it is a reaction against the ineffectual gradualism of social change, the faceless horror of technological society, and the myths perpetrated to distract us from the reality of impending universal cataclysm. In this latter period almost all American literature has an apocalyptic tone; the contemporary literary world seems genuinely to reflect a cultural climate that is itself universally apocalyptic. The climate, however, is turbulent; the literary processes are still no doubt in flux.

At its best, literature has always been known to imagine man in his totality. In nineteenth-century America, inclined to a romanticism that indulged national naiveté, the writers of fiction took a decidedly more realistic view of the human enterprise. Harry Levin has analyzed their exposure of that dark potential of the human heart lurking behind the smile of unending progress.[1] If the transcendentalists had forgotten the sinful past of our race and thus were inclined to project an innocent future for self-reliant man, Hawthorne acknowledges the defect of the human heart that inclines us to conceal our real selves from others. Imagining a variation of

Brook Farm—one of the more famous utopian experiments that reflected a secularized millenarianism—Hawthorne shows the illusory nature of such a quest for the ideal. It is illusory because it is based on a masquerade that refuses to acknowledge the murderer in each of us. Hawthorne's apocalypse is drawn in terms of the tragic end of a limited experiment; yet his revelation of the human heart is universally significant. Whatever ideal can be achieved by man must be approached realistically—with the prior acknowledgment of the murderer in each of us.

Melville reduces the case for optimism to its absurdity by loosing a disguised Satan on mid-nineteenth-century America. The confidence man either dupes the passengers of the *Fidèle* into placing false trust in him or reveals that they are beyond being duped because they are already inhuman. If Melville is truly saying, as we have suggested, that the Christian ideal of charity is impracticable, no firmer No could have been uttered in response to the millenarian expectations of the century. For it was Christian love that from the time of the Quakers on was supposed to transform the nation and the world.

Twain in *The Mysterious Stranger* reflects the bitter old age of a critic of that century of industrial expansion. His criticism cuts clear through any layers of optimism that may have remained, to the very core of the problem of human existence as he sees it. Not only is man incapable of improving his situation, his very essence as man that makes moral choice possible leads *de facto* to a preponderance of wrong choices. The proliferation of evil results in inevitable human misery. The only possible happiness is to be found in apocalyptic laughter—laughter that denies any reality to human existence other than the reality of illusion. *Maya* alone is salvation.

During this first phase the scope of the apocalyptic imagination is social. Hawthorne uses the image of experimentation in communal living but nevertheless makes a general statement about the human heart and the process of creative change. Melville writes dramatically about American types of the mid-nineteenth century. The cataclysm he imagines is muted; the extinction of a light signals the end as one would darken a stage at the end of a play. Even though his types are American, his judgment of Christianity is total. Twain uncharacteristically and deceptively stages his tale of youthful initiation into *maya* in an Austria still in the Middle Ages. His images are global, his judgment of human existence complete.

The second phase of American literary apocalypse as represented here by Faulkner, West, and O'Connor places emphasis on the individual. American history during the first half of the twentieth century, despite our involvement in two world wars, seems predominantly a period of isolationism and introspection. The focal point of the period is the Great Depression, and the attention of the nation was necessarily directed toward the widespread human misery that it caused. This national experience clearly affected the imagination of Nathanael West. Faulkner and O'Connor are products of a Southern culture that, economically at least, lags behind the rest of the country; its literature, for reasons still intriguing literary historians, is highly developed in relation to our national literature. Southern literature, regional in tone and mood, is nonetheless universal in its human appeal. In Faulkner and O'Connor there is an emphasis on the individual in relation to transcendent values that we will consider characteristic of this second period. O'Connor, it is true, wrote after mid-century; in the scope of her apocalypse, however, she is closer to Faulkner and West than to contemporary apocalyptists.

Death is central to the Judeao-Christian treatment of apocalypse; it is the dark moment of truth for the individual that yields new life for those judged worthy of the kingdom. And although we will have to delay assessment of West's place in the apocalyptic tradition, it is clear that death is judgment in his novel *Miss Lonelyhearts* just as pointedly as it is revealer in *As I Lay Dying* and *The Violent Bear It Away*.

In Faulkner and O'Connor death is the source of creative revelation. Addie Bundren's death is the agent of judgment for herself and her family. The endured ordeal of her death and burial yields new life, with the modesty of existence itself, for Cash only. In *The Violent Bear It Away*, Mason's death begins the week of apocalyptic initiation for Tarwater. Death is Mason's passage into the true life of his heavenly country. The bread of life that satisfies man's hunger totally can be eaten, paradoxically, only after one dies. Tarwater, in the aftermath of his great-uncle's death, submits to a *rite de passage* that teaches him this very truth—that the hunger he experiences can be satiated only by his own death. Responding to grace, he accepts a life shorn of its accidentals and reaches monomaniacally for the mercy of the kingdom. Miss Lonelyhearts' death, on the other hand, is at best a simple judgment of his connivance in the ultimate illusion of man—to appoint oneself savior of mankind. Nathanael West knows the misery of human existence; he is convinced of the necessity of illusion for man if he is to survive suffering. The apocalypse imagined by West is the necessary and empty consequence of man's futile attempt to escape his situation.

The third phase of American apocalyptic literature is roughly confined to the period after 1950. It is a time of national awakening to the disease of racial injustice and, internationally, of *angst* and alienation resulting from the human displacement of the last world war. It is a period of cold-war tension, of the proliferation of nuclear potential, of the exploration of space. It is, in short, a period of technological plenty amid mythological poverty. The sense of loss of world has intensified rapidly since mid-century; it has produced a new breed of apocalyptic response. These writers find the world so absurd that their apocalypse is laced with despair and laughter. The laughter is designed either to ease the pain of adjustment to a better world or to accompany the acceptance of life's joke. Their imagery is predominantly social, as distinguished from the emphasis on the individual in the previous period. Apocalypse at present is a reflection of the climate of the age rather than a reaction against it, as was the case with the nineteenth-century authors.

The climate of increased racial tension in mid-century America is for Ellison in *Invisible Man* a metaphoric setting for his parable about the depersonalization of modern society. Man is invisible today, Ellison says, because he has been used by others and has surrendered himself to their use. Baldwin in *Go Tell It on the Mountain* writes about the everyday life of the Negro in America a century after emancipation. The victim of white America's religion that counsels patience in suffering, the American Negro waits only to be emancipated from the oppression of Christianity. Nothing will replace that faith; there will be then only the emptiness of a wasted dream—the American dream of equality among men. Baldwin's muted apocalypse describes in vividly human terms the futility of belief in new life. For Richard Wright the American ghetto is a microcosm of the universal oppression of minority groups. Like Baldwin, Wright uses the symbolism of new creation for ironic effect. The only way the oppressed American black can develop a sense of personal dignity is through creative violence. The American black thus typifies oppressed man who dies for the violent assertion of self at the hands of an oppressor who must take revenge in order to maintain his own selfhood.

The social dimension of apocalypse is continued in the works of the humorous apocalyptists. Primary concern extends beyond specifically national problems; the catastrophe that is anticipated or imagined is the result of the ideological and technological breakdown of modern society. The settings of Barth and Pynchon are American, but there is nothing to prevent us from understanding their works as reflective of the general cultural malaise of today's world. Vonnegut imagines the destruction of the whole world by ice—through American ingenuity; yet he is writing basically about the pretensions of technological and religious man.

John Barth parodies the ideologies of contemporary man and shows how, reduced to the absurdity of absolutes, they paralyze man like the serpents of Laocoön. Existentialism, the myth of the hour, is his primary target. Humor lightens the realization that, as an absolute, existentialism is far more dangerous apparently than the old eternal verities. Thomas Pynchon views the absurdity of the California megalopolis. His latter-day Oedipus, a woman, inherits the land; but even at the end of the story we are as unsure as she about what she has actually inherited. The expected revelation may be that a massive system of evil supports the frenzy of modern life. Of all of the novelists considered here, Vonnegut is the only one actually to stage the final cataclysm. With the persuasion of a dedicated *wrang-wrang*, he freezes the world in the very act of laughing at itself and its pretensions. The world has sought to save itself through invention and has found only a convenient way to "cool it" forever.

In the novels of the first period there does not seem to be any strong sense of the movement of history. Imagining history from creation through the final revelation, Mark Twain seems to be dealing with a sequence that is fundamentally closed. At any rate, man in his view is essentially the same from beginning to end. Melville, perhaps because of the limitations of his static setting, seems rather to be announcing the essential impracticability of the Christian ideal than to be observing America reach a point of disintegration. Movement in the novel is limited to the mutations of the confidence man's disguises and the changes of place necessitated by the journey down the Mississippi. Hawthorne alone shows awareness of the passage of time; and although on a superficial level the last condition of Hollingsworth, Priscilla, and Coverdale is worse than the first—their experiment has failed—there is the deeper level of growth and insight on which Hollingsworth at least is a richer human being. In the second phase, there is awareness of the passage of time in Faulkner and O'Connor, but it is a history in terms of the individual. They are concerned with the effects of time upon the individual as he perceives salvation and damnation. West reverts to the essentialistic pattern of Twain and Melville, at least insofar as he tells of necessary human frustration. The writers of the third phase are aware of a moment in time that can be distinguished from the preceding; the present is worse than the past because of the accumulation of offenses against human dignity.

II

The typology of apocalypse that was projected in chapter 1 must now be sharpened to include the variations and innovations of American literary apocalypse. On the basis of an investigation of primitive religious myths and of the Judaeo-Christian understanding of the Eschaton, we established the threefold scheme of traditional apocalypse, constituted by the symbolism of judgment, catastrophe, and renewal. Primitive and Judaeo-Christian apocalypse, each manifesting the three constitutive elements, are differentiated on the basis of their norm for judgment and view of history. Primitive apocalypse judges the present on the basis of the past and accepts a cyclic view of history. In Judaeo-Christian apocalypse, time is irreversible and the norm for judging the present is the coming kingdom. The difference between the two lies primarily, therefore, in the elements of judgment and renewal. Through a survey of two centuries of American expectation of the kingdom, we bridged the gap between traditional or classical apocalypse and nineteenth-century secular millenarianism. The utopian concept emasculated traditional apocalypse by anticipating a millennium without catastrophe and for that reason, as we have seen, should not be considered apocalyptic at all.

Although none of the novels that I have taken account of seems to typify the cyclic view of renewal that is characteristic of primitive apocalypse, there are three adaptations of the primitive symbolism of judgment and catastrophe. *The Blithedale Romance* employs the imagery of paradise, specifically of Eden, as a humorous counterpoint to the utopian endeavors of the Blithedale community. The imagery is a product of Coverdale's descriptive fancy as narrator; and although it undoubtedly serves to highlight the failure of Blithedale, it cannot be taken as a serious indication of Hawthorne's preference for the past as a norm for the renewal of the present. Any attempt to achieve the ideal, Hawthorne asserts, must repudiate the masquerade of mutual deception; it must begin with the reality of our propensity to exploit others. It seems beyond question that Hawthorne did not believe in the redemptive value of Christ's death; his imagination, steeled in the school of education through sinful experience, nevertheless seems open to a future that is qualitatively superior to the past. The new life that results from the acknowledgment of the darkness in our hearts is indeed genuinely new. The past for Hawthorne is not, therefore, something to return to; its heritage of sin must be recognized and, if possible, repudiated. In *The Blithedale Romance*, Hawthorne uses the imagery of paradise as humorous irony; the hope projected by his imagination is basically Judaeo-Christian.

The ritual return to chaos, constituting the basis of regeneration, is typical of the primitive imagination. West in *Miss Lonelyhearts* works with images of chaos in American life. Nature, the works of man, and human misery are all symbolic of the chaos of existence. It is this chaos that Miss Lonelyhearts—the priestess of twentieth-century America—must impose order upon. Yet despite the presence of the primitive symbols of order and chaos, there is no hope in the world of Miss Lonelyhearts. In *As I Lay Dying*, Faulkner's principal images are fire and water, both primitive symbols of the chaos that yields life.

West and Faulkner, although functioning on one level within the framework of primitive apocalypse, employ imagery that is Christian. Central to West's novel is the motif of Miss Lonelyhearts' temptation by Shrike on analogy to Christ's conflict with the devil in the desert. The water and fire in *As I Lay Dying* are transformed into Christian symbols of initiation and salvation, even though in Addie's mind they remain merely the signs of her salvation from Anse by Jewel. Thus, to complete our discussion of these two works, we must take into consideration the sequence of Christian apocalyptic symbolism.

In *As I Lay Dying*, as in many of the great Puritan apocalyptic treatises, the death of the individual is the moment of apocalypse, both end and judgment. The circumstances related to Addie's death and burial, concentrated in the ordeals by water and fire, become also a *rite de passage* for the Bundren family. Cash alone, however, seems to grow as a result of the revelation death has brought. His humane concern for Darl and his sensitivity to the complexity of human relationships signify a genuine transformation of consciousness; Addie's death has given birth to a totally new awareness in him. Faulkner's novel focuses primarily on the moments of death and judgment; the emphasis is on the individual in relation to this apocalyptic rhythm of existence. His imagination is Christian in its openness to the future, yet realistic in its awareness of the agonizingly slow process of change.

Although death occurs finally as judgment in *Miss Lonelyhearts*, the emphasis in the novel—despite the importance of order and chaos as symbols—is on the warning signs preceding the end. Shrike as tempter is a type of the loosed Satan of traditional Christian apocalypse. Shrike is literally a secular refraction of the Christian Satan; however, the pattern of his temptation of

Miss Lonelyhearts is so clearly derived from the Gospels, it seems appropriate to characterize West's imagination here as consciously Christian. Philip Traum in Twain's *The Mysterious Stranger* is without qualification the loosed Satan of the Christian imagination. Yet, despite the fact that each of these novels uses imagery that is Christian, the scope of the imagination in neither case is ultimately Christian; i.e., open to a future that is genuinely new. West, through the interrelationship of Shrike and Miss Lonelyhearts, speaks paradoxically of man's need for illusion; although man cannot live without his dreams, when pushed to the extreme the dreams lead inevitably to death. Twain makes his loosed Satan the savior of Theodor Fischer, in a blasphemous reversal of the Christian gospel. The Good News is that salvation comes only through the denial of reality.

Both *The Violent Bear It Away* and *Go Tell It on the Mountain* focus on images of new life, specifically of the heavenly kingdom, yet for almost diametrically opposed reasons. The hunger that Mason educates Tarwater to recognize is a hunger for life that can be satisfied only by the bread of life in the kingdom. Tarwater is repelled by this dream of fulfillment that Mason believes in. Yet, when he finally accepts the mission that he is called to, he looks at Powderhead and sees an eternal hillside where a throng is being fed from a single basket and Mason is waiting to share the loaves and fishes. Tarwater acknowledges his hunger as a tide within himself and knows that it will be satisfied finally only if he spends his life preaching "the terrible speed of mercy."[2]

Flannery O'Connor's apocalyptic imagery creates a mood of mystery, the expectation of the totally new. Her imagination is patently Christian.

In *Go Tell It on the Mountain*, the Sunday morning following John Grimes's dark night of faith is the first day of the new creation; and the images of the bright, clear streets of the Heavenly Jerusalem are taken directly from the Book of Revelation. In the final analysis, though, the novel cannot be read simply on the literal level of a young Negro's experience of God's saving grace. The images of the eternal city that his joy projects upon the New York slum are defeated by the very mood of the novel. The experience described is indeed genuine, but the implication of the whole tone of the novel is that the experience will not last. Faith cannot protect John from the agony of living in a divided country. Despite the use of the Christian images of renewal, Baldwin writes about a future that is ultimately hopeless.

In three instances—*The Mysterious Stranger*, *Miss Lonelyhearts*, and *Go Tell It on the Mountain*—we have already noted the use of Christian symbolism drained of its rhythm of hope. *The Mysterious Stranger* uses Christian images for an antichristian purpose. The new life that is suggested is not life at all; it is the acceptance of illusion with laughter. *Miss Lonelyhearts* offers simply death and judgment. It is man's fate apparently to accept the inevitability of misery. *Go Tell It on the Mountain* employs images of hope only as the superficial consolation of a phase in the life of youth; John's passage through night's womb of guilt has left nothing really

changed. The experience of faith is just something else
to be rejected in the process of a Negro's awakening to
white domination. This is indeed one significant variation on apocalyptic form in American literature—the
use of traditional Christian images of apocalypse, even
of new life, but drained of hope.

Where the traditional apocalyptic symbols are transformed into a secular or worldly analogue, we are dealing with American literary innovations in apocalypse. I
refer specifically to the transformation of the loosing of
Satan into the advent of the confidence man and the
conversion of cosmic destruction or death as a spiritual
reality into the emptiness of strikes, riots, bombings, and
wars—those man-made disruptions of civil and international life. The norm of judgment is some human
ideology against which man is considered defective; this
ideology is often heresy from a religious perspective. All
secular apocalypse is one in the absence of any clear
vision of the future of man; however, as we shall see,
one can believe in the future without necessarily being
able to imagine it. The secular apocalypse that seems
positively to deny the possibility of a future has been
tentatively called the apocalypse of despair, and it is this
innovation in apocalypse that must now be considered
in detail.

The Confidence-Man is undoubtedly the definitive
secular variation on the traditional image of the loosed
Satan. Melville's masterful evocation of the confidence
man in his multiple disguises is, moreover, the seminal
inspiration for a distinctive strand of American apocalypse, dedicated to the protean existence of the super-

promiser who heralds the dawn of doom.[3] Melville sees
mid-nineteenth-century America as the prey of false
doctrine precisely because the *vera doctrina* is impracticable. Man is created to be duped. Although there is
considerable humor in Melville's "work of amusement,"[4]
as he calls it, the total effect of a world in which one cannot win under any circumstance is frightening. And if
despair is too strong a word to characterize our reaction
to that world in which the last light has been extinguished, then Melville has at least gently imparted a
sense of hopelessness.

Gentleness is poles apart from the tone that marks
Richard Wright's apocalypse in *Native Son*. The end
Wright envisions is one of secular doom; the warning
sign is the mounting tension between the races. The cold
white world excites, paradoxically, the heat of violent
passion in Bigger Thomas. There is of course tragic irony
in the necessity of violence for creating the person who
must die because of his creation. Wright's vision springs
from despair; he can imagine no future. Destruction is
the inevitable end of a world in which violence is the
necessary instrument of creative selfhood, for oppressor
as well as oppressed.

Nevertheless, the strain of secular apocalypse is not
all gloom and depression, nor is the absence of affirmation
in the secular universally true. There is a tradition for
whimsical apocalypse in American literature that,
according to R. W. B. Lewis, goes all the way back to
The Confidence-Man—a development that we have
already noted. Yet, to consider *The Confidence-Man*,
The Mysterious Stranger, and *Miss Lonelyhearts* humor-

ous apocalypse, as Lewis does, is to focus too narrowly on words rather than on total effect. I have endeavored to justify the exclusion of Melville, Twain, and West from the strain of apocalyptic laughter, while conceding to Lewis the debt that the recent humorous apocalyptists owe to those three.

With recent humorous apocalypse a curious development takes place in which a minimal hope that is genuinely human remains, even though the imagination is specifically neither primitive nor Judaeo-Christian. Its norm for judgment is drawn from current humanism, and its hope is based on psychological necessity rather than a religious faith. It is fundamentally a wish that man will prevail, that somehow we can show our fellow man the minimal respect that is necessary to keep us from destroying each other. The traditional symbolism of apocalypse is present in its secular analogue. The last loosing of Satan is drawn in terms of the con man; the cataclysm is a product of technological intelligence and personal stupidity. Common to humorous apocalypse is the absence of a vision of the new. Its absence is not necessarily a denial of its possibility; rather it is a simple admission at most of the present impossibility of imagining one. Through an affirmation of some saving quality in man, humorous apocalypse does affirm the future; it simply refrains from imagining it concretely.

John Barth's *The End of the Road* falls within the broad scope of the secular apocalyptic imagination. Although the novel emphasizes the element of judgment—the futility of existentialism as an absolute—it also employs the image of the con man in the person of

Horner's doctor. The humor of obvious parody makes it impossible for us to classify it as apocalypse of despair, despite the fact that the final portion of the novel lapses into unintelligible realism. Like *The Crying of Lot 49*, it would seem to be in a twilight zone between despair and the affirmation of humorous apocalypse. Pynchon searches modern society for meaning and discovers a convergence of evidence that can be explained either by appeal to paranoia or as the revelation of transcendent evil. He operates within the framework of the warning signs of impending revelation; the confidence man is depersonalized into myriad clues related to a possible source of transcendent evil. The mood of his novel is one of intense expectation; yet Pynchon, like life, reserves the final revelation. He neither imagines a future nor denies its possibility. Nor does he seem to affirm any quality in man positively capable of contribution to survival. Powerless man awaits the unveiling.

Kurt Vonnegut's creation of the *wrang-wrang* typifies the affirmative thrust of the most recent American variation in apocalypse. *Cat's Cradle* projects the end of the world in a singularly imaginative way, and it is undoubtedly Vonnegut's faith in man alone that makes it possible for him to take such a close look at the end itself. Vonnegut knows the pretensions that have created the overwhelming sense of impending disaster, and as *wrang-wrang* he forces us to consider nothing sacred but man. Ralph Ellison in *Invisible Man* imagines with great humor the time just before the end in order to create a sense of urgent expectation; he too finds at least a spark of love in man that hopefully will put an end to the

depersonalization fostered by the pressures of modern
life. As blues artist Ellison sings passionately about the
agony of a faceless world and thereby imposes some slight
order on the chaos of a world of mutual exploitation.

It is possible now to see the inadequacy of certain
definitions of apocalypse, too narrowly linked to what
we have called traditional apocalypse. Walter Wink, in
words similar to those of Amos Wilder, asserts that apocalypse signals the end of one world and the beginning
of a new one. "Apocalypticism arises," he writes, "as a
result of the cracks that form under men's feet at those
moments in history when the times divide, and apocalypticism is literally visionary: it is the awful perception of
the end of that 'world' and the vision of the coming of
a new."[5] And Walker Percy, offering "Notes for a Novel
About the End of the World," says that "the novelist
writes about the coming end in order to warn about
present ills and so avert the end."[6] Percy's perspective is
probably best taken as a statement of personal imperative rather than as a description of the apparent purposes
of actual apocalyptic literature. There are writers, as
we have seen, who announce the coming end simply
because they discern its inevitability and apparently derive release from the anguish of their despair, in telling
it. Wink's description does justice to the traditional
apocalypse of primitive religion and Judaeo-Christianity, but it asks too much of secular apocalypse. Excep-
tion must certainly be made for the apocalypse of despair, if not also for humorous apocalypse, insofar as the
latter does not envision the new world concretely.
Wink's definition does not apply either to that use of

Christian images drained of hope which we have found in Twain, West, and Baldwin. Yet it seems only fair to suggest that what Wink is attempting is a contemporary restatement of traditional apocalypse rather than an empirical study of the varieties of current apocalypse; his definition is obviously suited to this limited purpose.

More substantial contributions to the understanding of the relationship between apocalypse and literature have been made recently by Northrop Frye, Frank Kermode, and Thomas J. J. Altizer; they deserve somewhat fuller consideration. Frye and Kermode are concerned with apocalypse insofar as it bears upon literary theory, and Altizer considers the apocalyptic sensibility of modern writers as a confirmation of the dawning of radical eschatological awareness.

Northrop Frye treats apocalypse within the framework of his theory of myths. Myth in terms of narrative, he says, is "the imitation of actions near or at the conceivable limits of desire."[7] Undisplaced myth is concerned with gods and demons, representing two contrasting worlds, one desirable and the other undesirable. These extreme forms of myth he calls the apocalyptic and the demonic.[8] The apocalyptic world is usually identified with the heaven of accepted religious belief, the demonic world with hell. Frye offers five major categories of apocalyptic imagery: divine, human, animal, vegetable, and mineral. His source of apocalyptic imagery is the New Testament Book of Revelation. The specific apocalyptic images—"the one God and the one Man, the Lamb of God, the tree of life, . . . and the rebuilt temple"[9]—all converge, he asserts, in the concept of "Christ."

There are, moreover, three types of displaced myth operating within the extremes of the apocalyptic and the demonic, corresponding to the romantic, high mimetic, and low mimetic modes of Frye's historical criticism. The three intermediate structures of images, concerned with human variations, are mythic by analogy with the undisplaced myths of the divine and the demonic. Frye calls them the analogy of innocence, the analogy of nature and reason, and the analogy of experience.[10] Innocence is the immediate displacement from the apocalyptic, experience from the demonic.

Frye's organization of mythic images is certainly thorough; it is characteristic of his encyclopedic genius. Yet his approach to the theory of myths betrays the weakness of the philosophical bias that pervades his essays on criticism. His structures of mythic images are static; when he speaks of the movement of myth ("images in process"), it is merely in terms of cyclic movement as in the rhythm of the seasons. Moreover, he has limited the category of apocalypse to what we have viewed as simply one constituent element of traditional apocalypse, the moment of new life. And the new life that he chooses to illustrate, the so-called life of the gods, represents simply the ultimate in human desire. Between the extremes of the apocalyptic and the demonic (the desirable and the undesirable) are three levels of displaced myth that correspond to arbitrary stages in the progressive diminution of desire. Insofar as this organization of mythic images is based on what would seem to be a static conception of human desire, the pattern is radically antihistorical and thus quite divergent from the acceptance of history that I have considered essential to an analysis of apocalypse. Moreover, the five structures of myth correspond to Frye's five fictional modes, which are explicitly described as cyclic; this is further confirmation of the antihistorical bias of Frye's theory. His cyclic rhythm of unalterable variations is as inviolable as Plato's world of Ideas.

Frank Kermode in *The Sense of an Ending* relates literary fictions to a general theory of fictions. *Fiction* is the term that Kermode uses for the ways that we try to make sense of our world; his task as critic is "the lesser feat of making sense of the ways we try to make sense of our lives."[11] Myth for Kermode has nothing to do with the limits of desire as it does for Frye; myth is what happens to fictions, he says, "whenever they are not consciously held to be fictive. . . . Fictions are for finding things out, and they change as the needs of sense-making change. Myths are the agents of stability, fictions the agents of change. Myths call for absolute, fictions for conditional assent."[12] Fiction is also different from hypothesis, because hypothesis is subject to verification whereas fiction is known to be provisional and once it has served its purpose is disposable.

One of the principal fictions that man has for making sense of history, according to Kermode, is the apocalyptic fiction of the end. Apocalypse provides the end to the sequence that has its beginning in Genesis; the overall view of history, as I indicated in chapter 1, is characteristic of Judaeo-Christian apocalypse. It is man who is in the middle, seeking harmony between beginning and end. "The paradigms of apocalypse," Kermode asserts, "continue to lie under our ways of making sense of the world."[13] And although the end has lost for us its naive *imminence*, we may speak of it now as *immanent*.[14] The apocalyptic pattern continues to be useful as *form* in our literature of crisis. "The concords books arrange between beginning, middle, and end"[15] satisfy our vital interest in the structure of time.

Kermode's understanding of imagination is ultimately his link between the general theory of fiction and literary fictions. The imagination is "a form-giving power, . . . a maker of orders and concords. We apply it to all forces which satisfy the variety of human needs that are met by apparently gratuitous forms."[16] Whether or not we care to accept the forms, we learn them the way we learn language. The *as if* of literary fiction like the *as if* of apocalypse is the humanizing form that we cannot do without. The forms console, "even perhaps bless us."[17] "If they mitigate our existential anguish it is because we weakly collaborate with them, as we collaborate with language in order to communicate."[18] Our "clerkly scepticism" preserves our fictions from becoming myths by revising them in answer to our changing experience, just as predictions of the end are constantly revised in the face of disconfirmation.

The elements of apocalypse that Kermode discusses in some detail are what he calls "certain arbitrarily chosen aspects of apocalyptic thinking and feeling."[19] They are Terrors, Decadence and Renovation, Transition, and

Clerkly Scepticism. I have less difficulty, though, with Kermode's analysis of these aspects of apocalypse than with his understanding of the purpose of apocalypse. To say that apocalypse conveys the "sense of an ending" is, first of all, to make too closed a structural pattern of the apocalyptic mode of thought. It makes the even more integral "sense of a beginning" seem to be the effect of the disconfirmation of apocalyptic prediction rather than a constituent element of apocalyptic thought. Kermode, it seems to me, has confused the expectation of the end with the prediction of the end. The expectation of the end and of a new beginning is essential to traditional apocalypse; prediction was never more than a misunderstanding of genuine apocalyptic belief.

Moreover, to speak of apocalyptic fictions as a consolation to us is not necessarily a distortion of the meaning of traditional apocalypse; the reason Kermode advances for their consoling power, though, does seem to me at least to miss the mark. Apocalypse consoles, not because it conceals the terror of history within the pleasing form of an expected ending, but rather because it counsels genuine hope in a new beginning despite the ravages of irreversible time. Kermode's theory of the blessing of form-giving fiction is, therefore, diametrically opposed to the awareness of the "fall into history" that I see as essential to the meaning of traditional apocalypse. Kermode seems to suggest, however, that the forms that please us are not "merely the architecture of our own cells."[20] If his implication is that the disconfirmation of the end that prediction necessarily entails offers some deeper lesson to man about the nature of historical reality, then his interpretation is perhaps not too far removed from the one that I have proposed.

Altizer is the only one of these three major contributors to the recent literature on apocalypse who approaches his subject from a theological perspective. His understanding of apocalypse is inseparable from his radical theology of the death of God; in fact, he seems to imply that genuine apocalyptic faith is inconceivable without willing the death of God. For Altizer there is no dawn of a new apocalyptic age without the total darkness of the unequivocal manifestation of evil: "Only when hell is fully and wholly manifest as hell or darkness can paradise or light appear in its final and total form." [21] The unequivocal presence of the demonic opens up the possibility of the appearance of its opposite, the dawn of a new and glorious Jerusalem.[22] The hell that has come to dominate the sensibility of the modern artist reveals finally the "long hidden apocalyptic roots"[23] of Western literature. Thus, literature becomes an aid to, if not a sign of, the reawakening of the apocalyptic faith of the New Testament.

In an article pertinent to this discussion of apocalypse in the American novel, Altizer asks if we can accept the Ahab of *Moby-Dick* as "a personification of the eschatological destiny of America."[24] He insists that in the context of America "Ahab's mad quest for the white whale can be seen as faith's response to the death of God, wherein the man of faith becomes the murderer of God so as to make possible a historical actualization of God's death in Jesus, and thus an apocalyptic consummation of God's original self-sacrifice or self-negation."[25] The Christian who truly wills God's death, Altizer goes on to say, will actualize the New Eden in a new and universal humanity.

Altizer rivals Frye in the manner in which he has made literature serve the demands of a theoretical bias. Frye rejects genuine literary history in favor of a Platonic heaven of static categories and recurring modes. Altizer allows his preoccupation with the death of God to win out over literature and its autonomy. His treatment of *Moby-Dick* as a paradigm of American rebellion suits more the needs of his theology than the demands of the text. The novel itself hardly seems to go beyond the inevitable folly of striking out against the malignity of the universe. Nevertheless, Altizer's understanding of apocalypse is genuinely historical and, after a fashion, hopeful; the fashion is, of course, his understanding of the death of God. Yet, because he preserves these two essential characteristics of traditional apocalypse, I find myself in greater sympathy with his radical understanding of apocalypse than with either Frye's or Kermode's.

The strand of American literary apocalypse that we have investigated has proved rich in creative adaptation. Where American apocalypse is realistically hopeful, as in *The Blithedale Romance, The Violent Bear It Away,* and *As I Lay Dying*, it is fully aware of the "fall into history"—an awareness that we consider essential to the meaning of Judaeo-Christian apocalypse. It is indeed, in Lewis' words, "another 'rebirth of images,' another reanimating of those great and ancient archetypes by which Western man has periodically explained to himself the full range of his condition and the most spectacular of his expectations or terrors."[26] Lewis need not have used the qualifier "Western." Anyone who has relinquished the facile optimism of imminent release from the agony of living can face the terror of history and accept the frighteningly slow process of growth into the future. Anyone with genuine hope can face the gloom of man's potential for destruction and yet work for the final city of man. Writers Hawthorne, O'Connor, and Faulkner know the tradition they are a part of; they are masters of their medium enough to use it creatively.

From the beginning, however, the American tradition for literary apocalypse has manifested a tendency to use the traditional symbols, not to instill a realistic acceptance of the agony of history, but rather for the very purpose apocalypse seemed originally aimed at defeating—despair amid the ravages of time. Loss of faith and its attendant self-understanding alone can explain this dramatic shift in purpose. With the blight of secularization already attacking the roots of religious faith, it is not surprising that the literary imagination developed its own everyday analogue for the images of classical apocalypse. The secular images could be used to perpetrate the same despair, with less irony perhaps, but power nonetheless. Apocalypse of despair concentrates on "the perennial degenerative tendencies of human nature and . . . metaphors to gauge their enormity."[27] It took finally the overall sense of loss of world of contemporary America to provoke a new apocalyptic imagination that recreates man's capacity to look with hope upon his history of mistakes. Humorous apocalypse, adapting the secular analogue of the traditional sequence, asks man to take such a close look at catastrophe that only laughter will relieve the tension. Yet the laughter is itself at least a passage to the future.

Our literature, in the final analysis, is caught not simply between "the wrath and the laughter" that Lewis has noted, but rather between hope and despair, just as a century earlier American theology fluctuated between hope and presumption. A rebirth of genuine hope would not by any means imply a cyclic return to the remote past. For the complete acceptance of the "fall into history" that hope entails would be captured anew in some unique configuration of apocalpytic images. Contemporary theologians, as we observed, are already creating a new language of eschatology. Teilhard de Chardin speaks about the future in terms of personalization; Bultmann reminds us of the call to authentic existence; and Moltmann projects the universal future of the kingdom as a fulfillment of the promise of life, righteousness, and freedom. Whether this new language of Christian hope will strengthen the affirmative trend of humorous apocalypse cannot, of course, be predicted. The theologians of promise may be simply voices crying in the wilderness rather than heralds of a new dawn of authentic hope. The future, however, depends upon clarity of vision and the option taken. If Christian faith will not support a universal vision of the future, we can perhaps do no more than hope for a rebirth of meaning from the spontaneous recurrence of archetypal images of new life.

(For abbreviations for the following chart see p. 230)

TYPOLOGY OF APOCALYPSE

Kinds of Apocalypse		Judgment	Warning Signs	The End	New Life	Purpose
				Constitutive Elements — **CATASTROPHE**		
TRADITIONAL	PRIMITIVE	Paradise — BR	Evil Age	Chaos	Cyclic	Contact with Reality
TRADITIONAL	JUDAEO-CHRISTIAN	Coming Kingdom — TV	Last Loosing of Satan — ML — MS	AI → Death — Cataclysm	Linear — GT	Genuine Hope
SECULAR	ANTICHRISTIAN	Secular Ideology ("Heresy")	Last Loosing	Death	Illusory	Hopelessness
SECULAR	APOC. OF DESPAIR	Secular Ideology — ER — CL	Con Man — CM — CL	NS → Riots Violence	✕	Despair
SECULAR	HUMOROUS	Humanism — ER	Expectation Con Man — IM — CL	CC → Riots—Nuclear Destruction	Linear Potential	(Psychological) Hope

ABBREVIATIONS

AI   *As I Lay Dying* (Faulkner)
BR   *The Blithedale Romance* (Hawthorne)
CC   *Cat's Cradle* (Vonnegut)
CL   *The Crying of Lot 49* (Pynchon)
CM   *The Confidence-Man* (Melville)
ER   *The End of the Road* (Barth)
GT   *Go Tell It on the Mountain* (Baldwin)
IM   *Invisible Man* (Ellison)
ML   *Miss Lonelyhearts* (West)
MS   *The Mysterious Stranger* (Twain)
NS   *Native Son* (Wright)
TV   *The Violent Bear It Away* (O'Connor)

NOTES

NOTES TO CHAPTER ONE

1. Jürgen Moltmann, *Theology of Hope* (New York: Harper & Row, 1967), p. 335.

2. Cf. my article "Language-Event as Promise: Reflections on Theology and Literature," *Canadian Journal of Theology* 16, Nos. 3 and 4 (1970), pp. 129–39.

3. Perry Miller, *Errand into the Wilderness* (New York: Harper & Row, 1964), p. 238.

4. Mircea Eliade, *Myth and Reality* (New York: Harper & Row, 1968), pp. 54–55.

5. Mircea Eliade, *The Sacred and the Profane* (New York: Harper & Row, 1961), pp. 78–79.

6. Mircea Eliade, *Cosmos and History: The Myth of the Eternal Return* (New York: Harper & Row, 1959), pp. 91–92.

7. Mircea Eliade, *Myths, Dreams, and Mysteries* (New York: Harper & Row, 1967), p. 225.

8. *Ibid.*, p. 224.

9. *Ibid.*, pp. 80–81.

10. *Ibid.*, p. 226.

11. Mircea Eliade, *Images and Symbols* (New York: Sheed & Ward, 1952), p. 57.

12. Eliade, *Myths, Dreams, and Mysteries*, pp. 23–27.

13. Eliade, *Images and Symbols*, p. 12.

14. *Ibid.*

15. *Ibid.*

16. *Ibid.*, p. 20.

17. Eliade, *Myths, Dreams, and Mysteries*, p. 27.

18. Eliade, *Images and Symbols*, p. 25.

19. *Ibid.*, p. 18.

20. R. H. Charles, *Eschatology: The Doctrine of a Future Life in Israel, Judaism and Christianity* (New York: Schocken, 1963), pp. 178–81.

21. Eliade, *Cosmos and History*, p. 128.

22. Charles, *Eschatology*, p. 183.

23. William A. Beardslee, "Hope in Biblical Eschatology and in Process Theology," *Journal of the American Academy of Religion* 38 (1970), 232.

24. Gerhard von Rad, *Old Testament Theology*, vol. 2: *The Prophets*, (New York: Harper & Row, 1966), p. 303.

25. *Ibid.*, pp. 301–2.

26. Martin Buber, *Pointing the Way* (New York: Harper & Row, 1963), p. 203.

27 *Ibid.*, p. 198.

28. Beardslee, "Hope in Biblical Eschatology," p. 232.

29. N. Turner, "Revelation," in *Peake's Commentary on the Bible*, ed. Matthew Black and H. H. Rowley (London: Thomas Nelson and Sons, 1962), p. 1043.

30. Andre Feuillet, *The Apocalypse* (New York: Alba House, 1965), p. 66.

31. *Ibid.*, pp. 74–83.

32. Turner, "Revelation," p. 1043.

33. William A. Beardslee, *Literary Criticism of the New Testament* (Philadelphia: Fortress Press, 1970), p. 55.

34. Feuillet, *Apocalypse*, p. 63.

35. *Ibid.*, pp. 75–76.

36. Austin Farrer, *A Rebirth of Images: The Making of St. John's Apocalypse* (Boston: Beacon Press, 1963), pp. 86–87.

37. Amos N. Wilder, "The Rhetoric of Ancient and Modern Apocalyptic." Paper read before the American Academy of Religion, 1970, pp. 4–5. (Xeroxed.)

38. Eliade, *Myths, Dreams, and Mysteries*, p. 154.

39. *Ibid.*, p. 153.

40. Charles, *Eschatology*, p. 205.

41. Moltmann, *Theology of Hope*, p. 16.

42. *The New English Bible with the Apocrypha* (Oxford and Cambridge University Presses, 1970), Rev. 2:7.

43. Miller, *Errand into the Wilderness*, pp. 1–15.

44. Perry Miller, ed., *The American Puritans: Their Prose and Poetry* (New York: Doubleday, 1956), p. 83.

45. Miller, *Errand into the Wilderness*, p. 9.

46. Michael McGiffert, "American Puritan Studies in the 1960s," *William and Mary Quarterly* 27 (January 1970), 45.

47. *Ibid.*, p. 54.

48. Ernest Lee Tuveson, *Millennium and Utopia: A Study in the Background of the Idea of Progress* (New York: Harper & Row, 1964), pp. 24–28.

49. H. Richard Niebuhr, *The Kingdom of God in America* (Chicago: Willet, Clark, 1937), p. 26.

50. *Ibid.*, p. 47.

51. Miller, *Errand into the Wilderness*, p. 218.

52. Niebuhr, *Kingdom of God in America*, p. 51.

53. *Ibid.*, pp. 128–29.

54. *Ibid.*, p. 91.

55. *Ibid.*, p. 138.

56. *Ibid.*, p. 150.

57. *Ibid.*, p. 133.

58. *Ibid.*, p. 162.

59. *Ibid.*, p. 151.

60. *Ibid.*, p. 179.

61. *Ibid.*, p. 150.

62. *Ibid.*, p. 189.

63. Miller, *Errand into the Wilderness*, p. 221.

64. *Ibid.*, p. 233.

65. *Ibid.*, pp. 236–37.

66. Harry Levin, *The Power of Blackness* (New York: Vintage Books, 1960), p. 7.

67. R. W. B. Lewis, *Trials of the Word* (New Haven: Yale University Press, 1965), p. 185.

68. Lewis, "Days of Wrath and Laughter," *Trials of the Word*, pp. 184–235.

69. Eliade, *Images and Symbols*, p. 64.

70. Gaston Bachelard, *The Psychoanalysis of Fire*, trans. Alan C. M. Ross (Boston: Beacon Press, 1964), pp. 103–4.

71. *Ibid.*, p. 106.

72. Lewis, *Trials of the Word*, p. 189.

NOTES TO CHAPTER TWO

1. Nathaniel Hawthorne, *The Blithedale Romance* (New York: W. W. Norton, 1958), p. 27. Subsequent references noted in the text are to this edition.

2. Frederick C. Crews, "A New Reading of *The Blithedale Romance*," *American Literature* 29 (1957), 147–70.

3. Peter B. Murray, "Mythopoesis in *The Blithedale Romance*," *PMLA* 75 (1960), 591.

4. Perry Miller, ed., *The American Puritans: Their Prose and Poetry* (New York: Doubleday, 1956), p. 83.

5. *Ibid.*

6. Daniel G. Hoffman, *Form and Fable in American Fiction* (New York: Oxford University Press, 1965), p. 210.

7. *Ibid.*, pp. 214–15.

8. Frank Davidson, "Toward a Re-Evaluation of *The Blithedale Romance*," *New England Quarterly* 25 (1952), 376.

9. Miller, *The American Puritans*, p. 4.

10. *Ibid.*

11. *Ibid.*, p. 5.

12. Nathaniel Hawthorne, *Selected Tales and Sketches* (New York: Holt, Rinehart & Winston, 1967), p. 145.

13. *Ibid.*, p. 142. Italics mine.

14. *Ibid.*, p. 147.

15. *Ibid.*, p. 149.

16. Hoffman, *Form and Fable*, p. 213.

17. Miller, *The American Puritans*, p.82.

18. There is typically no unanimity of opinion among critics about the number of disguises assumed by the confidence man. However, critical opinion would seem conveniently to fall within three possibilities. One sees all eight personages from the deaf-mute to the cosmopolitan as disguises of the same confidence man. A second finds six disguises, with the deaf-mute representing Christ and Black Guinea the devil. The third position recognizes seven successive manifestations of the confidence man following the appearance of Christ as the deaf-mute. The range of opinions concerning the *number* of guises does not even touch upon the problem of the *manner* in which the successive manifestations of the confidence man are to be related.

19. R. W. B. Lewis, *Trials of the Word* (New Haven: Yale University Press, 1965), p. 67.

20. Herman Melville, *The Confidence-Man* (New York: New American Library, 1964), p. 9. Subsequent references noted in the text are to this edition.

21. James E. Miller, Jr., "*The Confidence-Man*: His Guises," *PMLA*, 74 (1959), 107.

22. Hoffman, *Form and Fable*, pp. 281, 312.

23. *Ibid.*, p. 287.

24. *Ibid.*, p. 306.

25. Cotton Mather, *Magnalia Christi Americana*; or, *The Ecclesiastical History of New-England*, vol. 2 (Hartford: Silas Andrus & Son, 1853), p. 541.

26. *Ibid.*

27. *Ibid.*, p. 544.

28. The novel was unfinished at the time of Twain's death; and it was not until his literary executor, Albert Bigelow Paine, "discovered" the final chapter that the story was eventually published in 1916. Without a final chapter the story undoubtedly lacks a sense of direction, yet critics have had trouble justifying the relationship between the unambiguous solipsism of the last chapter and the earlier development of the story. In *Mark Twain and Little Satan* (West Lafayette, Ind.: Purdue University Studies, 1963), John S. Tuckey establishes conclusively the *order* of Twain's composition of three distinct versions of the Satan story, that Bernard DeVoto had previously named—the Eseldorf Version, the edited text that was actually published; the Hannibal Version, describing the influence of a young Satan named "44" on Tom Sawyer and Huck Finn; and the Print Shop Version, concerned again with "44," but as the dream self of August Feldner. One of Tuckey's conclusions is that Paine's last chapter is actually the conclusion to the

Print Shop Version; but since the Eseldorf text was clearly the most developed manuscript, he made the necessary editorial changes so that the Print Shop conclusion would fit the Eseldorf story. His thesis seems to have had little impact on the present state of criticism of the novel; there is obvious need, therefore, for serious critical study of the manuscripts. The publication of *Mark Twain's Mysterious Stranger Manuscripts* (Berkeley: University of California Press, 1969), edited by William M. Gibson, will no doubt aid this process. The volume contains the three fragmentary versions, with notes concerning the appearance of the manuscripts and all emendations, cancellations, marginalia—and in whose handwriting. As interesting and informative as these textual investigations will be, though, perhaps criticism will in the final analysis simply have to accept Paine's 1916 version as a kind of literary "fortunate fall"—a masterful piece of editing and, because of its extraordinary power, a work of art in its own right.

29. Edwin S. Fussell, "The Structural Problem of *The Mysterious Stranger*," *Studies in Philology* 49 (1952), 95–104. His essay, published ten years before Tuckey's rejection of the last chapter, justifies the acceptance of the Paine conclusion on the grounds that Twain did after all write the chapter; whether he liked it or not, says Fussell, is beside the point.

30. Pascal Covici, Jr., *Mark Twain's Humor* (Dallas: Southern Methodist University Press, 1962), p. 227.

31. William C. Spengemann, *Mark Twain and the Backwoods Angel* (Kent, Ohio: Kent State University Press, 1966), p. 127.

32. Coleman O. Parsons, "The Background of *The Mysterious Stranger*," *American Literature* 32 (1960), 55–74.

33. Mark Twain, *The Mysterious Stranger and Other Stories* (New York: New American Library, 1962), p. 161. Subsequent references noted in the text are to this edition.

NOTES TO CHAPTER THREE

1. Robert Fitzgerald, Introduction to *Everything That Rises Must Converge*, by Flannery O'Connor (New York: New American Library, 1967), p. xii.

2. William Faulkner, *As I Lay Dying* (New York: Random House, 1957), pp. 42–43. Subsequent references noted in the text are to this edition.

3. Michael Millgate, *The Achievement of William Faulkner* (New York: Random House, 1963), p. 110.

4. *Ibid.*

5. *The New English Bible with the Apocrypha* (Oxford and Cambridge University Presses, 1970), Mt. 3:11; cf. also Lk. 3:16.

6. Cf. Floyd C. Watkins and William B. Dillingham, "The Mind of Vardaman Bundren," *Philological Quarterly* 39 (1960), 247–51.

7. *The New English Bible*, Mt. 7:21.

8. Irving Howe, *William Faulkner: A Critical Study* (New York: Random House, 1952), p. 112.

9. Nathanael West, *Miss Lonelyhearts and The Day of the Locust* (New York: New Directions, 1962), p. 32. Subsequent references noted in the text are to this edition.

10. Flannery O'Connor, *Three* (New York: New American Library, 1964), p. 306. Subsequent references noted in the text are to this edition.

11. P. Albert Duhamel, "The Novelist as Prophet,"

in *The Added Dimension: The Art and Mind of Flannery O'Connor*, ed. Melvin J. Friedman and Lewis A. Lawson (New York: Fordham University Press, 1966), p. 95.

12. Granville Hicks, "A Writer at Home with her Heritage," *Saturday Review* 45, May 12, 1962, p. 22.

13. On the question of Tarwater's freedom, see Robert O. Bowen, "Hope vs. Despair in the New Gothic Novel," *Renascence* 13 (1961), 147–52; Sumner J. Ferris, "The Outside and the Inside: Flannery O'Connor's *The Violent Bear It Away*," *Critique* 3 (Winter-Spring 1960), 11–19; Flannery O'Connor, *Mystery and Manners*, ed. Sally and Robert Fitzgerald (New York: Farrar, Straus & Giroux, 1969), pp. 116–17; Louis D. Rubin, Jr., "Flannery O'Connor and the Bible Belt," *The Added Dimension*, ed. Friedman and Lawson, pp. 60–66; Rainulf A. Stelzmann, "Shock and Orthodoxy: An Interpretation of Flannery O'Connor's Novels and Short Stories," *Xavier University Studies* 20 (March 1963), 4–21.

14. Stanley Edgar Hyman, *Flannery O'Connor* (Minneapolis: University of Minnesota Press, 1966), p. 24.

15. Carter W. Martin, *The True Country: Themes in the Fiction of Flannery O'Connor* (Nashville: Vanderbilt University Press, 1968), p. 61.

16. Sister Mariella Gable, "Flannery O'Connor—A Tribute," *Esprit* 8 (Winter 1964), 26–27.

17. O'Connor, *Mystery and Manners*, pp. 113–14.

18. Frederick J. Hoffman, "The Search for Redemption," in *The Added Dimension*, ed. Friedman and Lawson, p. 41.

NOTES TO CHAPTER FOUR

1. Ralph Ellison, *Invisible Man* (New York: New American Library, 1953), p. 428. Subsequent references noted in the text are to this edition.

2. Ralph Ellison, *Shadow and Act* (New York: New American Library, 1966), p. 181.

3. *Ibid.*, p. 177.

4. Ralph Ellison, quoted in R. W. B. Lewis, *Trials of the Word* (New Haven: Yale University Press, 1965), p. 220. Source not acknowledged.

5. Irving Howe, "James Baldwin: At Ease in Apocalypse," *Harper's*, September 1968, p. 92.

6. Steven Marcus, "The American Negro in Search of Identity," *Commentary*, November 1953, p. 459.

7. James Baldwin, *Go Tell It on the Mountain* (New York: Dell, 1965), p. 18. Subsequent references noted in the text are to this edition.

8. Marcus, *loc. cit.*

9. *Collected Poems of Robert Frost* (New York: Henry Holt, 1930), p. 268.

10. Richard Wright, *Native Son* (New York: Harper & Row, 1966), p. 16. Subsequent references noted in the text are to this edition.

11. James Baldwin, *The Fire Next Time* (New York: Dell, 1964), p. 47.

NOTES TO CHAPTER FIVE

1. Robert Scholes, "'Mithridates, he died old': Black Humor and Kurt Vonnegut, Jr.," *The Hollins Critic* 3 (October 1966), 5–6.

2. John Barth, *The End of the Road* (New York:

Bantam, 1969), p. 141. Subsequent references noted in the text are to this edition.

3. Thomas Pynchon, *The Crying of Lot 49* (New York: Bantam, 1967), p. 10. Subsequent references noted in the text are to this edition.

4. An alternate spelling of Tristero; the interchangeability of the spellings is without apparent reason.

5. John W. Hunt, "Comic Escape and Anti-Vision: The Novels of Joseph Heller and Thomas Pynchon," in *Adversity and Grace*, ed. Nathan A. Scott, Jr. (Chicago: University of Chicago Press, 1969), p. 91.

6. *Ibid.*, p. 110.

7. *Ibid.*

8. James D. Young, "The Enigma Variations of Thomas Pynchon," *Critique: Studies in Modern Fiction* 10 (Fall 1967), 72.

9. Kurt Vonnegut, Jr., *Cat's Cradle* (New York: Dell, 1966), p. 58. Subsequent references noted in the text are to this edition.

10. Scholes, "Black Humor and Kurt Vonnegut," p. 8.

11. *Ibid.*, p. 11.

12. *Ibid.*, pp. 5–6.

13. Loren Eiseley, *The Unexpected Universe* (New York: Harcourt, Brace & World, 1969), pp. 38–39.

14. William F. Lynch, *Christ and Prometheus* (Notre Dame, Ind.: University of Notre Dame Press, 1970), p. 119.

15. Herbert F. Smith, "Barth's Endless Road," *Critique* 6 (Fall 1963), 69.

NOTES TO CHAPTER SIX

1. Harry Levin, *The Power of Blackness* (New York: Vintage Books, 1960).

2. Flannery O'Connor, *Three* (New York: New American Library, 1964), p. 447.

3. Cf. R. W. B. Lewis, "Days of Wrath and Laughter," in *Trials of the Word* (New Haven: Yale University Press, 1965).

4. Herman Melville, *The Confidence-Man* (New York: New American Library, 1964), p. 190.

5. Walter Wink, "Apocalypse in Our Time," *Katallagete* 3 (Fall 1970), 16.

6. Walker Percy, "Notes for a Novel About the End of the World," *Katallagete* 3 (Fall 1970), 5.

7. Northrop Frye, *Anatomy of Criticism: Four Essays* (New York: Atheneum, 1968), p. 136.

8. *Ibid.*, p. 139.

9. *Ibid.*, pp. 141–42.

10. *Ibid.*, pp. 151, 153–154.

11. Frank Kermode, *The Sense of an Ending: Studies in the Theory of Fiction* (New York: Oxford University Press, 1967), p. 3.

12. *Ibid.*, p. 39.

13. *Ibid.*, p. 28.

14. *Ibid.*, p. 6.

15. *Ibid.*, p. 178.

16. *Ibid.*, p. 144.

17. *Ibid.*, p. 165.

18. *Ibid.*, p. 144.

19. *Ibid.*, p. 93.

20. *Ibid.*, p. 165.

21. Thomas J. J. Altizer, "Imagination and Apocalypse," *Soundings* 43 (1970), 408.

22. The apparent victory of the demonic in *The Confidence-Man, The Mysterious Stranger,* and *Miss Lonelyhearts* takes on a vastly different meaning from the perspective of Altizer's *coincidentia oppositorum.*

23. Altizer, "Imagination and Apocalypse," p. 403.

24. Thomas J. J. Altizer, "Theology and the Contemporary Sensibility," in *America and the Future of Theology,* ed. William A. Beardslee (Philadelphia: Westminster Press, 1967), p. 20.

25. *Ibid.,* p. 31.

26. Lewis, *Trials of the Word,* p. 206.

27. *Ibid.*

WORKS CITED

ALTIZER, THOMAS J. J. "Imagination and Apocalypse." *Soundings* 43 (1970), 398–412.

———. "Theology and the Contemporary Sensibility." In *America and the Future of Theology*, edited by William A. Beardslee, pp. 15–31. Philadelphia: Westminster Press, 1967.

BACHELARD, GASTON. *The Psychoanalysis of Fire*. Translated by Alan C. M. Ross. Boston: Beacon Press, 1964.

BALDWIN, JAMES. *The Fire Next Time*. New York: Dell Publishing Co., 1964.

———. *Go Tell It on the Mountain*. New York: Dell Publishing Co., 1965.

BARTH, JOHN. *The End of the Road*. New York: Bantam Books, 1969.

BEARDSLEE, WILLIAM A. "Hope in Biblical Eschatology and in Process Theology." *Journal of the American Academy of Religion* 38 (1970), 227–39.

———. *Literary Criticism of the New Testament*. Philadelphia: Fortress Press, 1970.

BOWEN, ROBERT O. "Hope vs. Despair in the New Gothic Novel." *Renascence* 13 (1961), 147–52.

BUBER, MARTIN. *Pointing the Way*. New York: Harper & Row, Publishers, 1963.

CHARLES, R. H. *Eschatology: The Doctrine of a Future Life in Israel, Judaism and Christianity*. New York: Schocken Books, 1963.

COVICI, PASCAL, JR. *Mark Twain's Humor*. Dallas: Southern Methodist University Press, 1962.

CREWS, FREDERICK C. "A New Reading of *The Blithedale Romance*." *American Literature* 29 (1957), 147–70.

DAVIDSON, FRANK. "Toward a Re-Evaluation of *The Blithedale Romance*." *New England Quarterly* 25 (1952), 374–83.

EISELEY, LOREN. *The Unexpected Universe*. New York: Harcourt, Brace & World, 1969.

ELIADE, MIRCEA. *Cosmos and History: The Myth of the Eternal Return*. New York: Harper & Row, Publishers, 1959.

———. *Images and Symbols: Studies in Religious Symbolism*. New York: Sheed & Ward, 1952.

———. *Myth and Reality*. New York: Harper & Row, Publishers, 1968.

———. *Myths, Dreams, and Mysteries*. New York: Harper & Row, Publishers, 1967.

———. *The Sacred and the Profane: The Nature of Religion*. New York: Harper & Row, Publishers, 1961.

ELLISON, RALPH. *Invisible Man*. New York: New American Library, 1953.

———. *Shadow and Act*. New York: New American Library, 1966.

FARRER, AUSTIN. *A Rebirth of Images: The Making of St. John's Apocalypse*. Boston: Beacon Press, 1963.

FAULKNER, WILLIAM. *As I Lay Dying*. New York: Random House, 1957.

FERRIS, SUMNER J. "The Outside and the Inside: Flannery O'Connor's *The Violent Bear It Away*." *Critique* 3 (Winter-Spring 1960), 11–19.

FEUILLET, ANDRE. *The Apocalypse*. New York: Alba House, 1965.

FITZGERALD, ROBERT. Introduction to *Everything That Rises Must Converge*, by Flannery O'Connor. New York: New American Library, 1967.

FRIEDMAN, MELVIN J., and LAWSON, LEWIS A., eds. *The Added Dimension: The Art and Mind of Flannery O'Connor*. New York: Fordham University Press, 1966.

FROST, ROBERT. *Collected Poems of Robert Frost*. New York: Henry Holt & Co., 1930.

FRYE, NORTHROP. *Anatomy of Criticism: Four Essays*. New York: Atheneum, 1968.

FUSSELL, EDWIN S. "The Structural Problem in *The Mysterious Stranger*." *Studies in Philology* 49 (1952), 95–104.

GABLE, SISTER MARIELLA. "Flannery O'Connor—A Tribute." *Esprit* 8 (Winter 1964), 26–27.

GIBSON, WILLIAM M., ed. *Mark Twain's Mysterious Stranger Manuscripts*. Berkeley: University of California Press, 1969.

HAWTHORNE, NATHANIEL. *The Blithedale Romance*. New York: W. W. Norton & Co., 1958.

———. *Selected Tales and Sketches*. New York: Holt, Rinehart & Winston, 1967.

HICKS, GRANVILLE. "A Writer at Home with Her Heritage." *Saturday Review*, May 12, 1962, pp. 22–23.

HOFFMAN, DANIEL G. *Form and Fable in American Fiction*. New York: Oxford University Press, 1965.

HOWE, IRVING. "James Baldwin: At Ease in Apocalypse." *Harper's*, September 1968, pp. 92–100.

———. *William Faulkner: A Critical Study*. New York: Random House, 1952.

HUNT, JOHN W. "Comic Escape and Anti-Vision: The Novels of Joseph Heller and Thomas Pynchon." In *Adversity and Grace*, edited by Nathan A. Scott, Jr., pp. 87–112. Chicago: University of Chicago Press. 1969.

HYMAN, STANLEY EDGAR. *Flannery O'Connor*. Minneapolis: University of Minnesota Press, 1966.

KERMODE, FRANK. *The Sense of an Ending: Studies in the Theory of Fiction*. New York: Oxford University Press, 1967.

LEVIN, HARRY. *The Power of Blackness*. New York: Vintage Books, 1960.

LEWIS, R. W. B. *Trials of the Word*. New Haven: Yale University Press, 1965.

LYNCH, WILLIAM F. *Christ and Prometheus*. Notre Dame, Ind.: University of Notre Dame Press, 1970.

McGIFFERT, MICHAEL. "American Puritan Studies in the 1960s." *William and Mary Quarterly* 27 (January 1970), 36–67.

MARCUS, STEVEN. "The American Negro in Search of Identity." *Commentary*, November 1953, pp. 456–63.

MARTIN, CARTER W. *The True Country: Themes in the Fiction of Flannery O'Connor*. Nashville: Vanderbilt University Press, 1968.

MATHER, COTTON. *Magnalia Christi Americana*; or, *The Ecclesiastical History of New-England*. Vol. 2. Hartford: Silas Andrus & Son, 1853.

MAY, JOHN R. "Language-Event as Promise: Reflections on Theology and Literature." *Canadian Journal of Theology* 16, Nos. 3, 4 (1970), pp. 129–39.

MELVILLE, HERMAN. *The Confidence-Man*. New York: New American Library, 1964.

MILLER, JAMES E., JR. "*The Confidence-Man*: His Guises." *PMLA* 74 (1959), 102–11.

MILLER, PERRY, ed. *The American Puritans: Their Prose and Poetry*. New York: Doubleday & Co., 1956.

———. *Errand into the Wilderness*. New York: Harper & Row, Publishers, 1964.

MILLGATE, MICHAEL. *The Achievement of William Faulkner*. New York: Random House, 1963.

MOLTMANN, JÜRGEN. *Theology of Hope*. New York: Harper & Row, Publishers, 1967.

MURRAY, PETER B. "Mythopoesis in *The Blithedale Romance*." *PMLA* 75 (1960), 591–96.

The New English Bible with the Apocrypha. Oxford and Cambridge University Presses, 1970.

NIEBUHR, H. RICHARD. *The Kingdom of God in America*. Chicago: Willett, Clark & Co., 1937.

O'CONNOR, FLANNERY. *Mystery and Manners*. Edited by Sally and Robert Fitzgerald. New York: Farrar, Straus & Giroux, 1969.

––––––. *Three*. New York: New American Library, 1964.

PARSONS, COLEMAN O. "The Background of *The Mysterious Stranger*." *American Literature* 32 (1960), 55–74.

PERCY, WALKER. "Notes for a Novel About the End of the World." *Katallagete* 3 (Fall 1970), 5–12.

PYNCHON, THOMAS. *The Crying of Lot 49*. New York: Bantam Books, 1967.

SCHOLES, ROBERT. "'Mithridates, he died old': Black Humor and Kurt Vonnegut, Jr." *The Hollins Critic* 3 (October 1966), 1–12.

SMITH, HERBERT F. "Barth's Endless Road." *Critique* 6 (Fall 1963), 68–76.

SPENGEMANN, WILLIAM C. *Mark Twain and the Backwoods Angel*. Kent, Ohio: Kent State University Press, 1966.

STELZMANN, RAINULF A. "Shock and Orthodoxy: An Interpretation of Flannery O'Connor's Novels and Short Stories." *Xavier University Studies* 20 (March 1963), 4–21.

TUCKEY, JOHN S. *Mark Twain and Little Satan*. West Lafayette, Ind.: Purdue University Studies, 1963.

TURNER, N. "Revelation." In *Peake's Commentary on*

the Bible, edited by Matthew Black and H. H. Rowley. London: Thomas Nelson and Sons, 1962.

TUVESON, ERNEST LEE. *Millennium and Utopia: A Study in the Background of the Idea of Progress*. New York: Harper & Row, Publishers, 1964.

TWAIN, MARK. *The Mysterious Stranger and Other Stories*. New York: New American Library, 1962.

VONNEGUT, KURT, JR. *Cat's Cradle*. New York: Dell Publishing Co., 1966.

VON RAD, GERHARD. *Old Testament Theology*. Vol. 2: *The Prophets*. New York: Harper & Row, Publishers, 1966.

WATKINS, FLOYD C., and DILLINGHAM, WILLIAM B. "The Mind of Vardaman Bundren." *Philological Quarterly* 39 (1960), 247–51.

WEST, NATHANAEL. *Miss Lonelyhearts and The Day of the Locust*. New York: New Directions Publishing Corp., 1962.

WILDER, AMOS N. "The Rhetoric of Ancient and Modern Apocalyptic." Paper read before the American Academy of Religion, 1970. Xeroxed, 10 pp.

WINK, WALTER. "Apocalypse in Our Time." *Katallagete* 3 (Fall 1970), 13–18.

WRIGHT, RICHARD. *Native Son*. New York: Harper & Row, Publishers, 1966.

YOUNG, JAMES D. "The Enigma Variations of Thomas Pynchon." *Critique* 10 (Fall 1967), 69–77.

INDEX